ATLAS of FIRSTS

Clive Gifford

KINGFISHER
NEW YORK

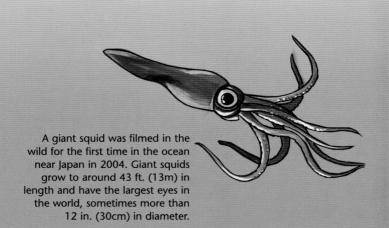

A giant squid was filmed in the wild for the first time in the ocean near Japan in 2004. Giant squids grow to around 43 ft. (13m) in length and have the largest eyes in the world, sometimes more than 12 in. (30cm) in diameter.

The World Bog Snorkeling Championships were first held in 1985. Competitors have to travel through 394 ft. (120m) of murky peat bog in Wales using flippers and a snorkel!

Contents

The world's first roads cleared by snowblowers were in the town of Outremont, near Montreal, Canada, in 1927, two years after the machine was invented by Arthur Sicard.

The first aviation disaster was in 1785 when a balloon crashed on the town of Tullamore in the Republic of Ireland, setting about 100 houses on fire.

Al-Jazari was the first engineer to record the moving parts of water clocks at the Artuklu Palace in Diyarbakir, Turkey. He wrote his *Book of Knowledge of Ingenious Mechanical Devices* in 1206.

Woolly mammoth remains about 20,000 years old were first discovered by nine-year-old Simion Jarkov near Novorybnoye, Russia, in 1997.

Simón Bolívar was named El Libertador in 1813 in Mérida after leading his first invasion of Venezuela in South America. He helped to free Venezuela, Ecuador, Bolivia, Colombia, and Peru from Spanish rule.

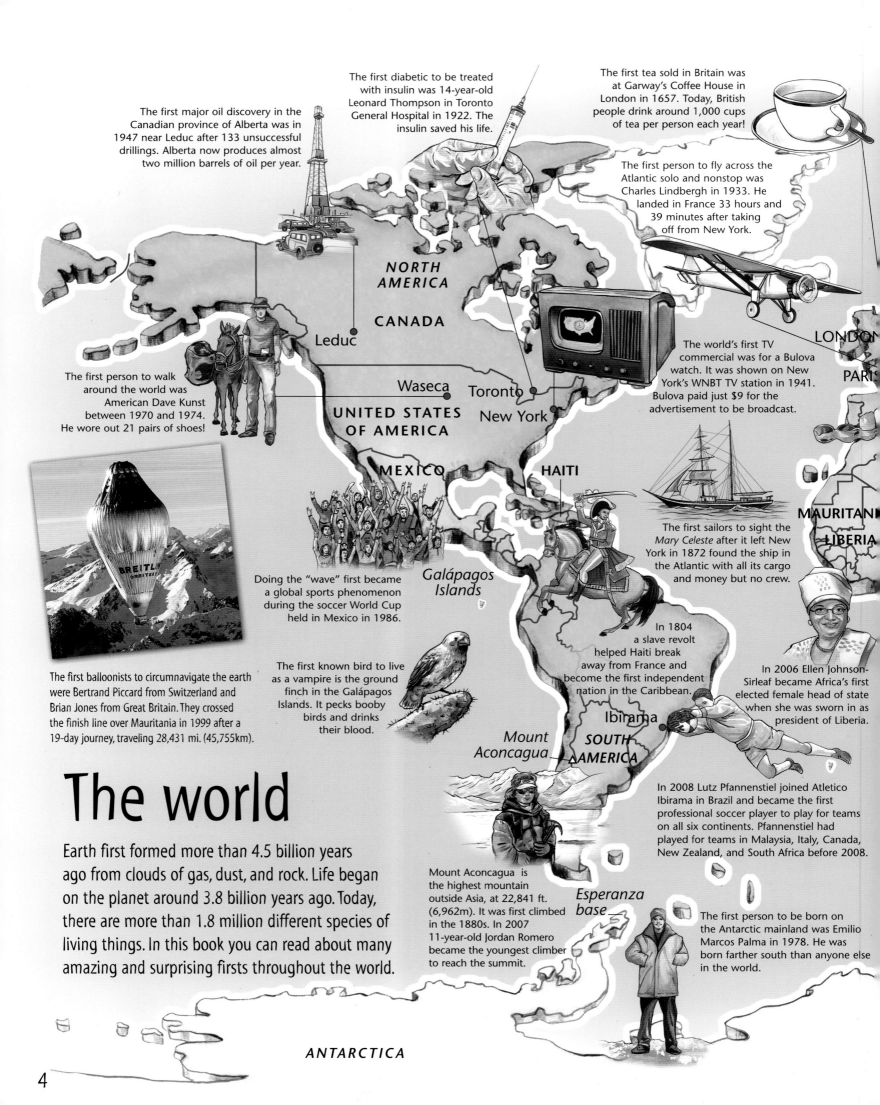

The first major oil discovery in the Canadian province of Alberta was in 1947 near Leduc after 133 unsuccessful drillings. Alberta now produces almost two million barrels of oil per year.

The first diabetic to be treated with insulin was 14-year-old Leonard Thompson in Toronto General Hospital in 1922. The insulin saved his life.

The first tea sold in Britain was at Garway's Coffee House in London in 1657. Today, British people drink around 1,000 cups of tea per person each year!

The first person to fly across the Atlantic solo and nonstop was Charles Lindbergh in 1933. He landed in France 33 hours and 39 minutes after taking off from New York.

NORTH AMERICA

CANADA

Leduc

The first person to walk around the world was American Dave Kunst between 1970 and 1974. He wore out 21 pairs of shoes!

Waseca   Toronto

New York

UNITED STATES OF AMERICA

The world's first TV commercial was for a Bulova watch. It was shown on New York's WNBT TV station in 1941. Bulova paid just $9 for the advertisement to be broadcast.

LONDON

PARIS

MEXICO   HAITI

The first sailors to sight the *Mary Celeste* after it left New York in 1872 found the ship in the Atlantic with all its cargo and money but no crew.

MAURITANIA

LIBERIA

Doing the "wave" first became a global sports phenomenon during the soccer World Cup held in Mexico in 1986.

Galápagos Islands

The first balloonists to circumnavigate the earth were Bertrand Piccard from Switzerland and Brian Jones from Great Britain. They crossed the finish line over Mauritania in 1999 after a 19-day journey, traveling 28,431 mi. (45,755km).

The first known bird to live as a vampire is the ground finch in the Galápagos Islands. It pecks booby birds and drinks their blood.

In 1804 a slave revolt helped Haiti break away from France and become the first independent nation in the Caribbean.

In 2006 Ellen Johnson-Sirleaf became Africa's first elected female head of state when she was sworn in as president of Liberia.

Ibirama

Mount Aconcagua

SOUTH AMERICA

In 2008 Lutz Pfannenstiel joined Atletico Ibirama in Brazil and became the first professional soccer player to play for teams on all six continents. Pfannenstiel had played for teams in Malaysia, Italy, Canada, New Zealand, and South Africa before 2008.

The world

Earth first formed more than 4.5 billion years ago from clouds of gas, dust, and rock. Life began on the planet around 3.8 billion years ago. Today, there are more than 1.8 million different species of living things. In this book you can read about many amazing and surprising firsts throughout the world.

Mount Aconcagua is the highest mountain outside Asia, at 22,841 ft. (6,962m). It was first climbed in the 1880s. In 2007 11-year-old Jordan Romero became the youngest climber to reach the summit.

Esperanza base

The first person to be born on the Antarctic mainland was Emilio Marcos Palma in 1978. He was born farther south than anyone else in the world.

ANTARCTICA

4

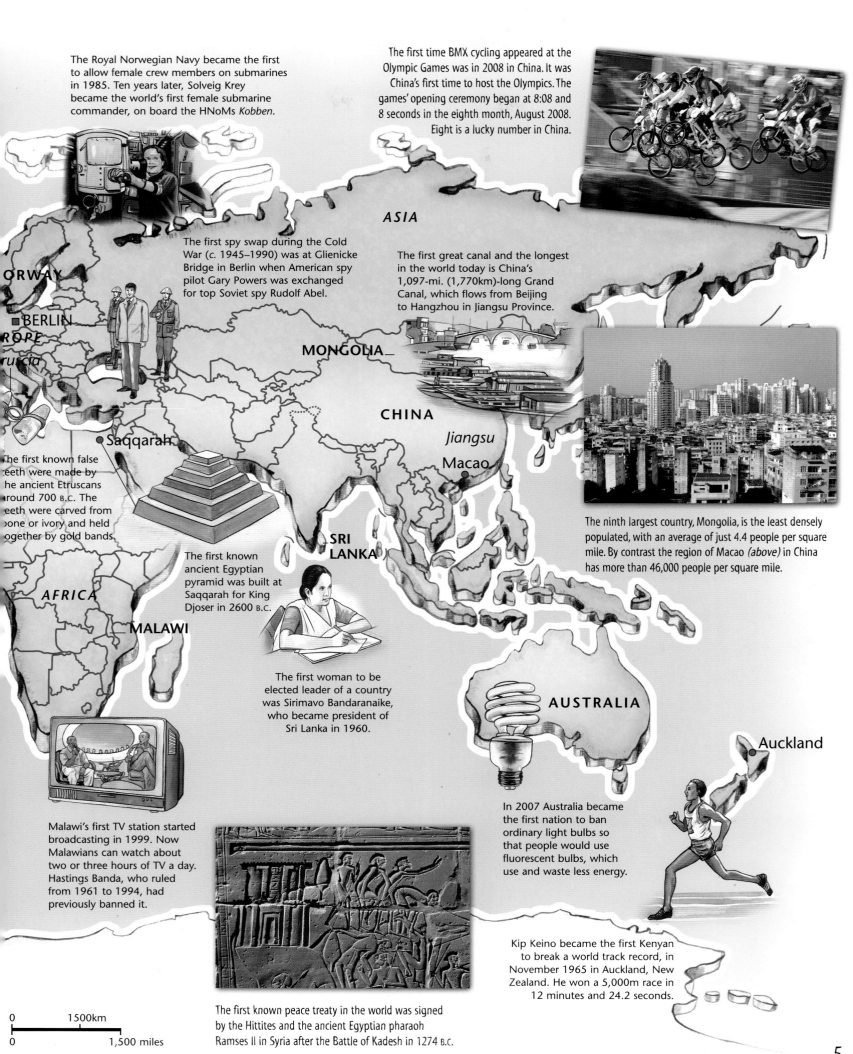

The Royal Norwegian Navy became the first to allow female crew members on submarines in 1985. Ten years later, Solveig Krey became the world's first female submarine commander, on board the HNoMs *Kobben*.

The first time BMX cycling appeared at the Olympic Games was in 2008 in China. It was China's first time to host the Olympics. The games' opening ceremony began at 8:08 and 8 seconds in the eighth month, August 2008. Eight is a lucky number in China.

ASIA

The first spy swap during the Cold War (*c.* 1945–1990) was at Glienicke Bridge in Berlin when American spy pilot Gary Powers was exchanged for top Soviet spy Rudolf Abel.

The first great canal and the longest in the world today is China's 1,097-mi. (1,770km)-long Grand Canal, which flows from Beijing to Hangzhou in Jiangsu Province.

ORWAY

BERLIN

ROPE

ussia

Saqqarah

MONGOLIA

CHINA

Jiangsu

Macao

The first known false teeth were made by the ancient Etruscans around 700 B.C. The teeth were carved from bone or ivory and held together by gold bands.

The ninth largest country, Mongolia, is the least densely populated, with an average of just 4.4 people per square mile. By contrast the region of Macao *(above)* in China has more than 46,000 people per square mile.

SRI LANKA

The first known ancient Egyptian pyramid was built at Saqqarah for King Djoser in 2600 B.C.

AFRICA

MALAWI

The first woman to be elected leader of a country was Sirimavo Bandaranaike, who became president of Sri Lanka in 1960.

AUSTRALIA

Auckland

Malawi's first TV station started broadcasting in 1999. Now Malawians can watch about two or three hours of TV a day. Hastings Banda, who ruled from 1961 to 1994, had previously banned it.

In 2007 Australia became the first nation to ban ordinary light bulbs so that people would use fluorescent bulbs, which use and waste less energy.

The first known peace treaty in the world was signed by the Hittites and the ancient Egyptian pharaoh Ramses II in Syria after the Battle of Kadesh in 1274 B.C.

Kip Keino became the first Kenyan to break a world track record, in November 1965 in Auckland, New Zealand. He won a 5,000m race in 12 minutes and 24.2 seconds.

0   1500km

0   1,500 miles

5

Eastern United States

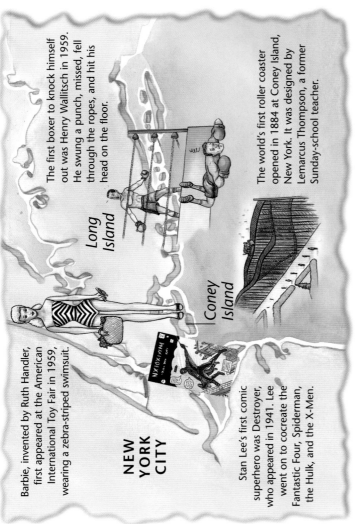

The largest city in the U.S., New York City, and the smallest state, Rhode Island, are both in the eastern part of the country. The U.S. Constitution was written and signed here in 1787. The region's southernmost city, Miami, was the first American city to be founded by a woman, Julia Tuttle, in the late 1800s.

```
0        100km
0              100 miles
```

KEY TO EAST COAST STATES
1 Maine
2 Vermont
3 New Hampshire
4 New York
5 Massachusetts
6 Rhode Island
7 Connecticut
8 Pennsylvania
9 New Jersey
10 Delaware
11 Maryland
12 Virginia
13 West Virginia

NEW YORK CITY

Barbie, invented by Ruth Handler, first appeared at the American International Toy Fair in 1959, wearing a zebra-striped swimsuit.

Long Island

The first boxer to knock himself out was Henry Wallitsch in 1959. He swung a punch, missed, fell through the ropes, and hit his head on the floor.

Coney Island

The world's first roller coaster opened in 1884 at Coney Island, New York. It was designed by Lemarcus Thompson, a former Sunday-school teacher.

Stan Lee's first comic superhero was Destroyer, who appeared in 1941. Lee went on to cocreate the Fantastic Four, Spiderman, the Hulk, and the X-Men.

Martha's Vineyard

Baseball's first World Series was held in 1903. The Boston Red Sox beat the Pittsburgh Pirates in the seven-game series.

● Boston

Ben Cohen and Jerry Greenfield opened their first ice cream store in Burlington in 1978. To celebrate their 20th year in 1998, they gave away 550,000 ice creams.

● Burlington   ● Nashua

Hartford ●

New York *(see inset)*

The first computer games console sold was the Magnavox Odyssey in 1972. Designed by Ralph Baer, it was black and white and had no sound.

The first person to cross Niagara Falls on a tightrope was Jean François Gravelot, or The Great Blondin, in 1859. Later that year he crossed again, carrying his manager.

Niagara Falls

Thomas Alva Edison *(below)* invented the first phonograph for recording and playing sound in 1877.

Detroit ●

The world's first mass-produced car was the first Model T Ford, launched in 1908. More than 15 million were made before production ended in 1927.

Ann Arbor ●

MICHIGAN

The first person to break three track and field world records in a single afternoon was Jesse Owens in 1935 in Ann Arbor.

WISCONSIN

The first Ferris wheel was named after inventor George W. Ferris. He built it for the 1893 World's Fair in Chicago. The wheel was moved to St. Louis, where it was blown up in 1960.

Chicago

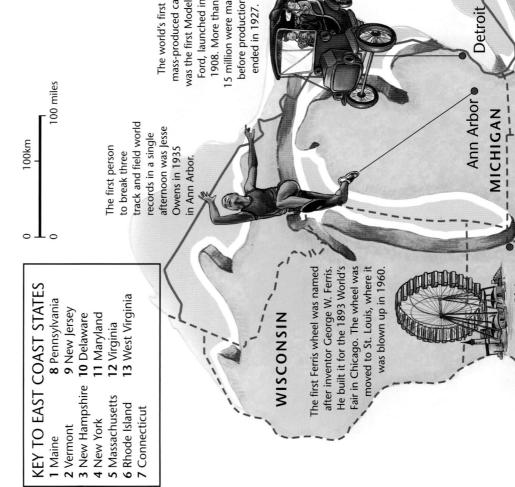
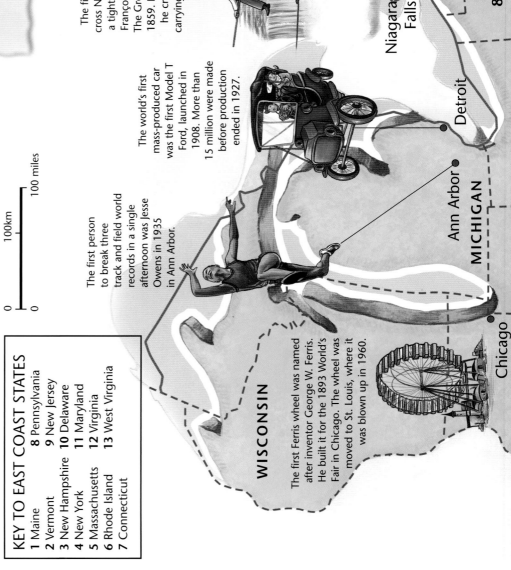

...blockbuster was *Jaws*, filmed on Martha's Vineyard. It won three Oscars, inspired three sequels, and earned more than $470 million.

William Gray invented the first coin-operated telephone in 1889. It was installed in Hartford Bank, and local calls cost five cents.

In 1903 the Wright Brothers made the first successful powered flight at Kill Devil Hill near Kitty Hawk.

The first child born in the American colonies was Virginia Dare in 1587. The colony on Roanoke Island was set up in 1584 by Sir Walter Raleigh.

Roanoke Island

Kitty Hawk

10
11

WASHINGTON, D.C.

Manassas
12

The first big land battle of the Civil War was the First Battle of Bull Run at Manassas in 1861.

The first NBA basketball player to score 100 points in a single game was Wilt Chamberlain of the Philadelphia Warriors, playing against the New York Knicks in 1962.

Christian "Jim" Roper won the first NASCAR race, on a dirt track at Charlotte Speedway in 1949. It was watched by 23,000 people.

Telephone pioneer Alexander Graham Bell invented the metal detector in 1881 to find the bullet in assassinated President James A. Garfield.

13

NORTH CAROLINA

Charlotte

SOUTH CAROLINA

Louisville

The first gorilla born in captivity was Colo, at Columbus Zoo in Ohio in 1956. In 1979 Colo became a grandmother.

The country music radio show *Grand Ole Opry* was first broadcast on October 5, 1925. The show is still going—it's the longest-running live radio program in the world.

GEORGIA

FLORIDA

Tampa

Canadian goalie Manon Rheaume was the first woman to compete in a men's professional ice hockey game, playing for the Tampa Bay Lightning in 1992.

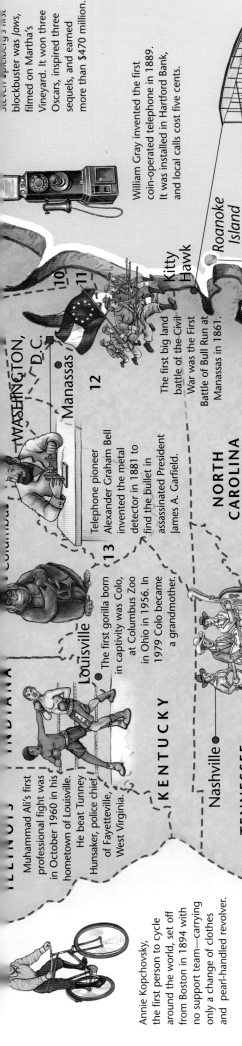

KENTUCKY

Nashville

TENNESSEE

Muhammad Ali's first professional fight was in October 1960 in his hometown of Louisville. He beat Tunney Hunsaker, police chief of Fayetteville, West Virginia.

Memphis

Tupelo

Tupelo-born Elvis Presley's first public performance was in a talent show at the 1945 Mississippi-Alabama Fair and Dairy Show. He was age 10.

ALABAMA

The first U.S. supermarket chain opened in Memphis in 1916. It was called Piggly Wiggly. Twenty years later, the chain introduced the first shopping carts at its Oklahoma City stores.

MISSISSIPPI

Annie Kopchovsky, the first person to cycle around the world, set off from Boston in 1894 with no support team—carrying only a change of clothes and pearl-handled revolver.

In 1862 the Battle of Antietam was the first major battle of the Civil War to be fought on territory held by the Union. About 23,000 men were killed, wounded, or listed as missing in action—more than in any other battle during the war.

Western United States

The western United States was first settled more than 12,000 years ago. During the 1800s, Native American tribes became outnumbered by the many pioneers and farmers who moved west in search of land and riches. The largest state in the west is Texas, while California has the most people. The Hollywood movie industry is based just outside Los Angeles, California's biggest city. Los Angeles's first movie theater opened in 1902.

0 — 300km

0 — 300 miles

The first Starbucks coffee house was opened in 1971 by two teachers and a writer. By 2008, the company had more than 15,000 stores.

WASHINGTON

Seattle

Mount St Helens △

In 1980 Mount St. Helens lost 1,312 ft. (400m) of height when it blew 500 million tons of ash over an area almost twice the size of Maryland.

OREGON

IDAHO

In 1997 ThrustSSC became the first land vehicle to break the sound barrier. It set a world land speed record of 763 mph (1,228km/h) in the Black Rock Desert.

The first permanent artificial heart transplant was in 1982 at the University of Utah Medical Center.

Black Rock Desert

In 2001 San Francisco Giants batter Barry Bonds hit his first home run against the San Diego Padres. By the season's end, he had hit 73 home runs, a Major League Baseball record.

NEVADA

Salt Lake City

San Francisco

CALIFORNIA

Chuck Yeager made the world's first supersonic flight over the Mojave Desert in 1947, reaching 670 mph (1,078km/h).

UTAH

The Hollywood sign was first put up in 1923. It was an ad for houses and spelled "Hollywoodland" until 1949, when "land" was removed.

HOLLYWOOD

Grand Canyon

The first Yukon Quest Sled Dog Race set out from Fairbanks, Alaska, in 1984. The 1,000-mi. (1,600km) race was won in just over 12 days by Sonny Lindner and his dogs.

ALASKA

Fairbanks

Mojave Desert

Hollywood

Los Angeles

San Diego

ARIZONA

The first in-flight refueling was in 1923. U.S. Air Force pilots later set a world record by flying for 37 hours over San Diego, refueling in the air.

The lava flow from a volcano was diverted by aerial bombing for the first time in 1935 to save the town of Hilo.

HAWAII

George Lucas and Steven Spielberg first discussed the Indiana Jones movies while making sandcastles at Mauna Kea in 1977. Indiana was Lucas's dog.

△ •Hilo
Mauna Kea

The first actor to insure her legs for a million dollars was Hollywood star Betty Grable. The Fox movie studio insured her legs with Lloyds of London.

In November 2008 Democratic Party candidate Barack Obama won the U.S. presidential election to become America's first African-American president and the first to be born in Hawaii. He is shown here with his family on the night of the election.

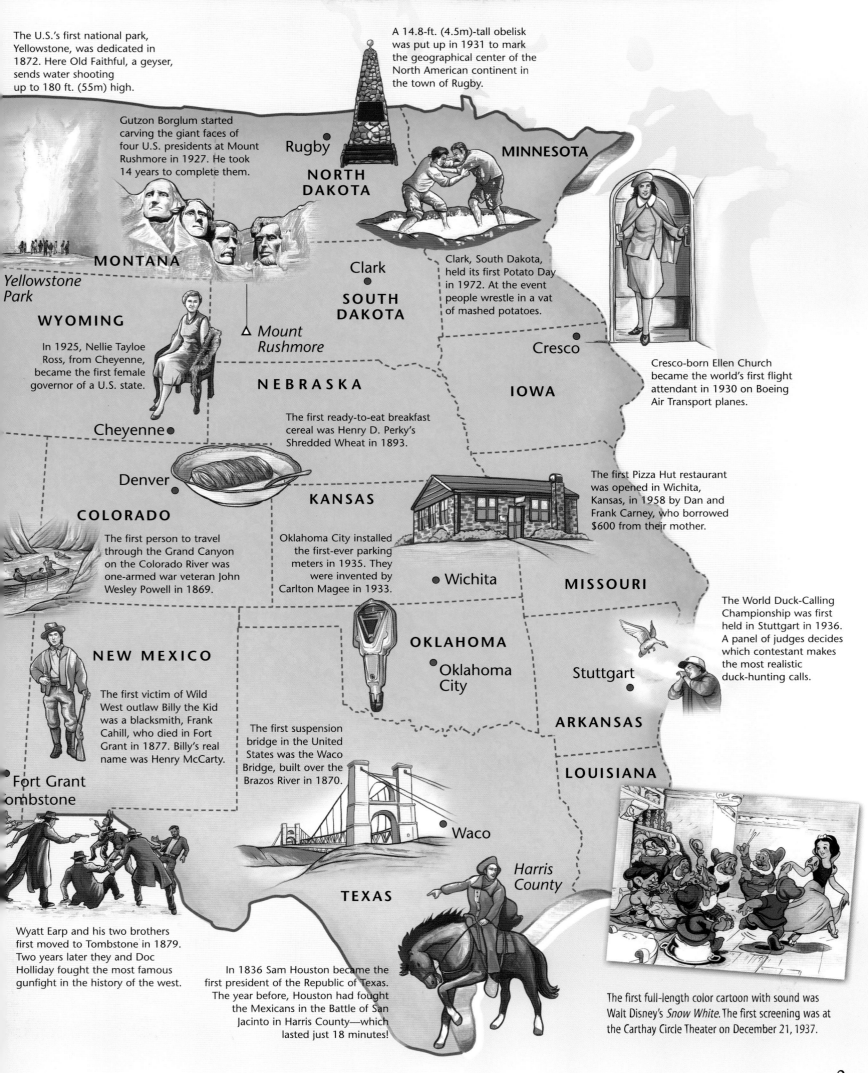

The U.S.'s first national park, Yellowstone, was dedicated in 1872. Here Old Faithful, a geyser, sends water shooting up to 180 ft. (55m) high.

A 14.8-ft. (4.5m)-tall obelisk was put up in 1931 to mark the geographical center of the North American continent in the town of Rugby.

Gutzon Borglum started carving the giant faces of four U.S. presidents at Mount Rushmore in 1927. He took 14 years to complete them.

Rugby

NORTH DAKOTA

MINNESOTA

MONTANA

Clark

Yellowstone Park

SOUTH DAKOTA

Clark, South Dakota, held its first Potato Day in 1972. At the event people wrestle in a vat of mashed potatoes.

WYOMING

△ Mount Rushmore

Cresco

In 1925, Nellie Tayloe Ross, from Cheyenne, became the first female governor of a U.S. state.

NEBRASKA

IOWA

Cresco-born Ellen Church became the world's first flight attendant in 1930 on Boeing Air Transport planes.

Cheyenne

The first ready-to-eat breakfast cereal was Henry D. Perky's Shredded Wheat in 1893.

Denver

KANSAS

The first Pizza Hut restaurant was opened in Wichita, Kansas, in 1958 by Dan and Frank Carney, who borrowed $600 from their mother.

COLORADO

The first person to travel through the Grand Canyon on the Colorado River was one-armed war veteran John Wesley Powell in 1869.

Oklahoma City installed the first-ever parking meters in 1935. They were invented by Carlton Magee in 1933.

Wichita

MISSOURI

The World Duck-Calling Championship was first held in Stuttgart in 1936. A panel of judges decides which contestant makes the most realistic duck-hunting calls.

NEW MEXICO

OKLAHOMA

Oklahoma City

Stuttgart

The first victim of Wild West outlaw Billy the Kid was a blacksmith, Frank Cahill, who died in Fort Grant in 1877. Billy's real name was Henry McCarty.

The first suspension bridge in the United States was the Waco Bridge, built over the Brazos River in 1870.

ARKANSAS

LOUISIANA

Fort Grant
ombstone

Waco

Harris County

TEXAS

Wyatt Earp and his two brothers first moved to Tombstone in 1879. Two years later they and Doc Holliday fought the most famous gunfight in the history of the west.

In 1836 Sam Houston became the first president of the Republic of Texas. The year before, Houston had fought the Mexicans in the Battle of San Jacinto in Harris County—which lasted just 18 minutes!

The first full-length color cartoon with sound was Walt Disney's *Snow White*. The first screening was at the Carthay Circle Theater on December 21, 1937.

Canada and the Arctic

Canada has more than 151,000 mi. (243,000km) of coast-line, more than any other country in the world. The highest tides in the world are at the Bay of Fundy, which separates New Brunswick from Nova Scotia. At some times of the year the difference between high and low tide is almost 56 ft. (17m)—the height of a three-story building.

The Klondike Gold Rush began in 1897, a year after gold was first discovered in Bonanza Creek. About 100,000 people trekked from other parts of North America to get rich.

Bonanza Creek

NORTHWEST TERRITORIES

The first sign in the Signpost Forest at Watson Lake was put up in 1942 by a homesick U.S. soldier, Carl K. Lindley, pointing toward his hometown. Others followed, and by 1990 there were 10,000 signs.

YUKON TERRITORY

Canada's largest national park, Wood Buffalo, was set up in 1922 and has about 5,000 buffalo—the world's biggest herd. The park is almost twice the size of Massachusetts.

Watson Lake

At 1,815.4 ft. (553.33m), the CN Tower is Canada's highest building and was first opened in 1976. In 1999, Ashrita Furman became the first person to climb the tower's 1,899 steps on a pogo stick!

BRITISH COLUMBIA

Wood Buffalo National Park

West Edmonton Mall opened in 1981 and is the biggest mall in North America. It has 800 stores and the world's biggest indoor water park.

Lewis Gordon Pugh became the first person to make a long-distance swim at the North Pole in July 2007. He swam 0.62 mi. (1km) in 19 minutes in freezing water.

Bathtub racing began with the Nanaimo to Vancouver World Championship in 1967. Competitors race along a 36 mi. (58km) course.

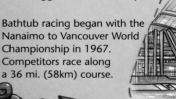

The first Polar Circle Marathon was run in 2001 over ice, snow, and unpaved tracks in western Greenland.

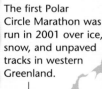

North Magnetic Pole

ARCTIC OCEAN

North Pole

Edmonton
ALBERTA

Calgary

Nanaimo

Cypress Hills

The first Calgary Stampede was a massive rodeo held in 1912 by Guy Weadick. It was the richest rodeo competition in North America, with $20,000 in prize money.

In 1774 Constantine Phipps was the first European to describe a polar bear in a book about his attempt to reach the North Pole.

Kangerlussuaq

Greenland

Nuuk

Norwegian Fridtjof Nansen and his team were the first to cross Greenland in 1888 when they reached Nuuk, Greenland's capital.

The Royal Canadian Mounted Police (Mounties) built their first fort at Cypress Hills in 1875. Today their national headquarters are in Ottawa.

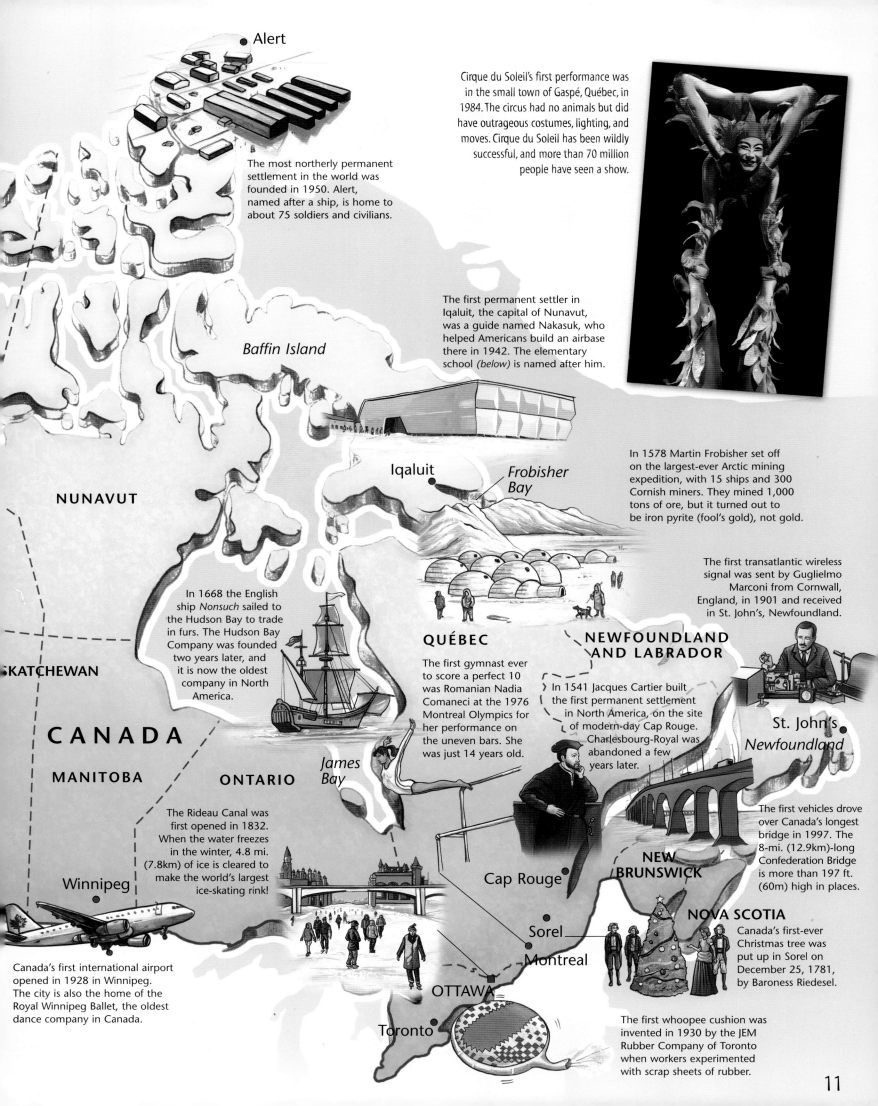

Alert

The most northerly permanent settlement in the world was founded in 1950. Alert, named after a ship, is home to about 75 soldiers and civilians.

Cirque du Soleil's first performance was in the small town of Gaspé, Québec, in 1984. The circus had no animals but did have outrageous costumes, lighting, and moves. Cirque du Soleil has been wildly successful, and more than 70 million people have seen a show.

Baffin Island

The first permanent settler in Iqaluit, the capital of Nunavut, was a guide named Nakasuk, who helped Americans build an airbase there in 1942. The elementary school *(below)* is named after him.

NUNAVUT

Iqaluit

Frobisher Bay

In 1578 Martin Frobisher set off on the largest-ever Arctic mining expedition, with 15 ships and 300 Cornish miners. They mined 1,000 tons of ore, but it turned out to be iron pyrite (fool's gold), not gold.

In 1668 the English ship *Nonsuch* sailed to the Hudson Bay to trade in furs. The Hudson Bay Company was founded two years later, and it is now the oldest company in North America.

The first transatlantic wireless signal was sent by Guglielmo Marconi from Cornwall, England, in 1901 and received in St. John's, Newfoundland.

...KATCHEWAN

QUÉBEC

The first gymnast ever to score a perfect 10 was Romanian Nadia Comaneci at the 1976 Montreal Olympics for her performance on the uneven bars. She was just 14 years old.

NEWFOUNDLAND AND LABRADOR

In 1541 Jacques Cartier built the first permanent settlement in North America, on the site of modern-day Cap Rouge. Charlesbourg-Royal was abandoned a few years later.

St. John's
Newfoundland

CANADA

MANITOBA

ONTARIO

James Bay

The Rideau Canal was first opened in 1832. When the water freezes in the winter, 4.8 mi. (7.8km) of ice is cleared to make the world's largest ice-skating rink!

The first vehicles drove over Canada's longest bridge in 1997. The 8-mi. (12.9km)-long Confederation Bridge is more than 197 ft. (60m) high in places.

NEW BRUNSWICK

Winnipeg

Cap Rouge

NOVA SCOTIA

Sorel

Canada's first-ever Christmas tree was put up in Sorel on December 25, 1781, by Baroness Riedesel.

Montreal

Canada's first international airport opened in 1928 in Winnipeg. The city is also the home of the Royal Winnipeg Ballet, the oldest dance company in Canada.

OTTAWA

Toronto

The first whoopee cushion was invented in 1930 by the JEM Rubber Company of Toronto when workers experimented with scrap sheets of rubber.

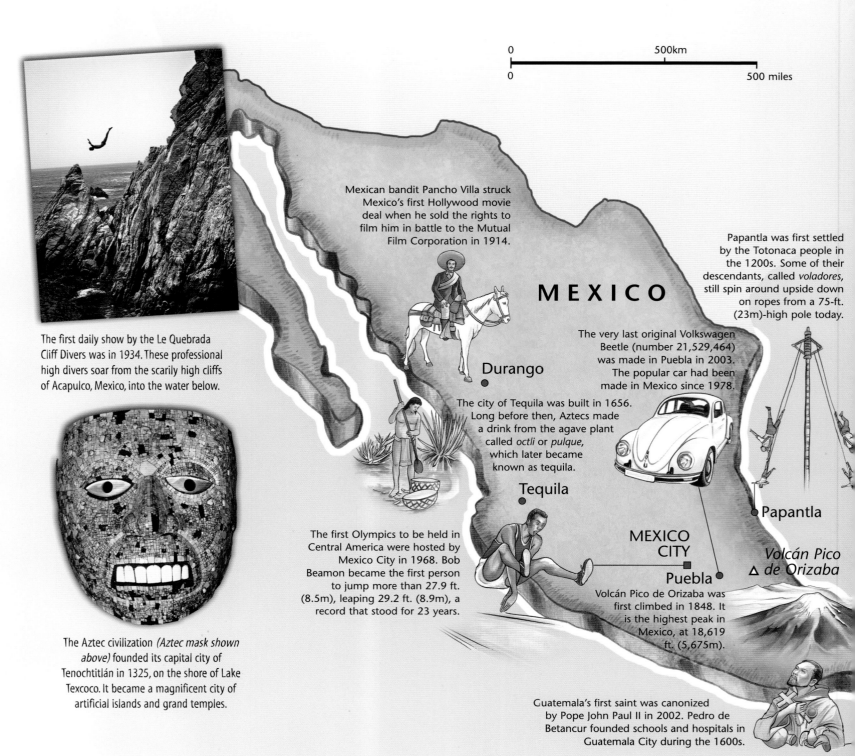

Mexican bandit Pancho Villa struck Mexico's first Hollywood movie deal when he sold the rights to film him in battle to the Mutual Film Corporation in 1914.

MEXICO

Papantla was first settled by the Totonaca people in the 1200s. Some of their descendants, called *voladores*, still spin around upside down on ropes from a 75-ft. (23m)-high pole today.

The first daily show by the Le Quebrada Cliff Divers was in 1934. These professional high divers soar from the scarily high cliffs of Acapulco, Mexico, into the water below.

The very last original Volkswagen Beetle (number 21,529,464) was made in Puebla in 2003. The popular car had been made in Mexico since 1978.

Durango

The city of Tequila was built in 1656. Long before then, Aztecs made a drink from the agave plant called *octli* or *pulque*, which later became known as tequila.

Tequila

The first Olympics to be held in Central America were hosted by Mexico City in 1968. Bob Beamon became the first person to jump more than 27.9 ft. (8.5m), leaping 29.2 ft. (8.9m), a record that stood for 23 years.

MEXICO CITY

Puebla

Papantla

Volcán Pico △ de Orizaba

Volcán Pico de Orizaba was first climbed in 1848. It is the highest peak in Mexico, at 18,619 ft. (5,675m).

The Aztec civilization *(Aztec mask shown above)* founded its capital city of Tenochtitlán in 1325, on the shore of Lake Texcoco. It became a magnificent city of artificial islands and grand temples.

Guatemala's first saint was canonized by Pope John Paul II in 2002. Pedro de Betancur founded schools and hospitals in Guatemala City during the 1600s.

Mexico, Central America and the Caribbean

There were several ancient civilizations in this region, including the Maya and the Aztecs, before European explorers arrived here in the 1400s. Mexico, in the north, is the world's 14th-largest country. Seven smaller countries make up Central America, and there are hundreds of islands, large and small, in the Caribbean Sea.

MEXICO 70

El Salvador first qualified for the soccer World Cup in June 1970, beating Honduras. The two nations later fought a short, brutal war known as the soccer war.

BAHAMAS

The first national park on Inagua was created in 1965. The nature sanctuary on Great Inagua Island is home to 80,000 West Indian flamingos—the largest flock in the world.

The first known Europeans to eat a pineapple were Christopher Columbus and his crew when they landed in Guadeloupe in 1493.

CUBA

Camagüey

Carlos Finlay, who was born in Camagüey, was the first person to suggest that the deadly disease yellow fever was transmitted by mosquitoes.

Inagua Islands

Ocho Rios

HAITI

DOMINICAN REPUBLIC

Puerto Rico

Guadeloupe

JAMAICA

Sam Lord built his lavish mansion in the 1820s with the profits of his piracy. He hung lanterns to lure ships onto the reef near his home.

James Bond's first movie mission was in the 1962 movie *Dr. No*, filmed mainly in Jamaica. The author of the Bond books, Ian Fleming, lived in Jamaica on an estate called Goldeneye.

Remy Bricka was the first person to walk across the Atlantic on ski floats. He went from Tenerife to Trinidad, arriving in May 1998.

Eugenia Charles became the first female leader of a Caribbean country in 1980. She governed as prime minister of Dominica until 1995.

DOMINICA

BARBADOS

TRINIDAD & TOBAGO

Hernan Cortez first landed on the coast of Mexico in 1519. He led a band of Spanish conquistadors to the Aztec capital ruled by Montezuma and captured the city in 1520.

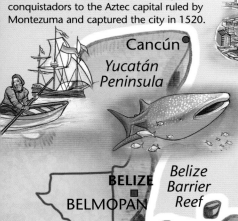

Cancún's first hotel was built in 1970 when only three people lived there. Today, Cancún is home to 600,000 people and has 150 hotels.

The first cricketer to score 400 runs in a test match innings was Brian Lara, playing for the West Indies against England in Antigua in 2004. His innings included four sixes and 43 fours.

Cancún

Yucatán Peninsula

The Belize Barrier Reef first became a UNESCO World Heritage site in 1996. The 186-mi. (300km) reef has 500 species of fish, including the whale shark, which can weigh 16 tons.

Copán is a ruined Mayan city abandoned by the Maya by A.D. 1200 and discovered by Spanish explorer Diego García de Palacio in 1570.

BELIZE

Belize Barrier Reef

BELMOPAN

GUATEMALA

GUATEMALA CITY

HONDURAS

Copán

TEGUCIGALPA

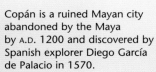

The first ship to travel through the Panama Canal between the Atlantic and Pacific oceans was the SS *Ancon* on August 15, 1914. The canal shortened journeys by thousands of miles.

SAN SALVADOR

EL SALVADOR

In 2001 the pygmy three-toed sloth was discovered in the swamps of Isla Escudo de Veraguas—the first new sloth discovered in the 21st century.

MANAGUA

NICARAGUA

Isla Escudo de Veraguas

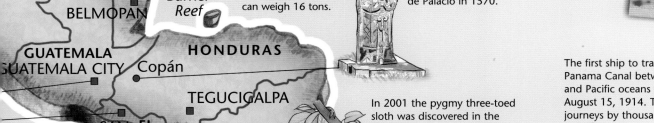

The first European to see the Pacific Ocean was Vasco Núñez de Balboa in 1513. He trekked through thick jungle in Panama to find the Pacific.

Monteverde

SAN JOSÉ

Panama Canal

PANAMA CITY

COSTA RICA

PANAMA

The earliest footprints in the Americas were found by builders in 1874. The footprints at Acahualinca, near Managua, are 6,000 years old.

The last golden toad was found at Monteverde in 1989. The toad became extinct in 2004 because of pollution, global warming, and habitat destruction.

South America and Antarctica

South America is the fourth-largest continent and has the world's biggest river and rainforest, the Amazon. Its biggest country is Brazil, where 370 million people live. By contrast, no one lives permanently in Antarctica, although hundreds work at research stations there, and more than 12,000 tourists visit each year.

The region of Lloro is probably the wettest place in the world. Every year an average of 524 in. (13,300mm) of rain falls there.

Jefferson Pérez from Cuenca became Ecuador's first Olympic gold medallist in 1996 when he won the 20km racewalking event.

Simón Bolívar was named El Libertador in 1813 in Mérida after leading his first invasion of Venezuela. He helped to free Venezuela, Ecuador, Bolivia, Colombia, and Peru from Spanish rule.

The largest swimming pool in the world is the San Alfonso del Mar seawater pool in Algarrobo, Chile. It is 3,323 ft. (1,013m) long and was completed in 2006.

The world's highest waterfall is Angel Falls, where the water drops 3,212 ft. (979m) into the Kerep River. Latvian explorer Aleksandrs Laime was the first to reach the falls on foot in 1955.

The first spacecraft launched from France's spaceport at Kourou was the DIAL satellite, sent into space by a Diamant-B rocket in March 1970.

The Amazon forest is full of world records. It has the largest beetle, the largest moth, the largest freshwater fish, and the smallest monkey, the pygmy marmoset, which is 6 in. (15cm) long and weighs just 3.5 oz. (100g).

The first people to escape from the prison colony on Devil's Island were Frenchman Henri Charrière and fellow prisoner Sylvain, who escaped using a bag of coconuts as a raft.

The first known waterproof raincoat was made in the late 1740s when François Fresneau coated an old coat with liquid rubber from trees.

Brazil's first coffee plantation was planted after Brazilian officer Francisco de Melo Palheta smuggled coffee seeds from French Guiana in 1727.

Mount Cotopaxi is 19,642 mi. (5,987m) high and has one of the only glaciers found near the equator. It is an active volcano and has erupted 50 times since the 1730s.

The huge Central Suriname Nature Reserve was first set up in 1998. It is home to giant armadillos, monkeys, and 500 species of birds.

In 1981 a ferry capsized at the port of Óbidos and 170 people were reported killed by piranhas, the world's most ferocious freshwater fish.

In 1911 American historian Hiram Bingham was the first to rediscover the ruined Inca city of Machu Picchu, on a mountain peak in the Andes.

Map labels

QUITO
Mount Cotopaxi
Cuenca
ECUADOR
Lloro
■BOGOTA
COLOMBIA
Mérida
VENEZUELA
CARACAS
GEORGETOWN
GUYANA
PARAMARIBO
SURINAME
Kourou
FRENCH GUIANA
Approuague
Devil's Island
Belem
Óbidos
BRAZIL
Angel Falls

The world's smallest newspaper was first published by Dolores Schwindt in 2000. *Vossa Senhoria* is a tiny 16-page monthly newspaper that measures 1 in. (2.54cm) by 1.4 in. (3.56cm).

The huge statue of Christ the Redeemer in Rio de Janeiro was first unveiled in 1931. The statue is 130 ft. (39.6m) high. Its head weighs 39.2 tons and the hands 10 tons each.

Pelé scored during his first game for Santos in 1956 and played soccer for the team until 1974. He scored an incredible 1,089 goals in matches for Santos.

Adauto Kovalski de Silva of Curitiba wrote his first book at just five years old. It was called *Learning Is Easy* and was published in October 2005.

The first dinosaur fossil found in Antarctica was *Antarctopelta oliveroi* in 1986. The four-legged skeleton was about 13 ft. (4m) long.

Founded in 1956, McMurdo Station is Antarctica's largest community. More than 1,000 people live there in the summer.

The coldest temperature measured on Earth was –128°F (–89°C) at Vostok on July 21, 1983.

Vostok

McMurdo base

ANTARCTICA

Rothera base

James Ross Island

The first person killed by a seal was a scientist dragged underwater by a large leopard seal near Rothera research station in 2003.

In 1993 a soccer referee sent off 20 players after a fight between General Caballero and Sportivo Ameliano—the most players ever sent off in a soccer league game.

The Itaipu hydroelectric power station first made electricity in 1984. The dam is 23,737 ft. (7,235m) long and as high as a 65-story building.

Divinópolis

Rio de Janeiro

Santos

BRASÍLIA

Itaipu

Curitiba

France's Lucien Laurent scored the first goal of the first soccer World Cup in 1930, in the 19th minute of the first game. France beat Mexico 4–1.

URUGUAY

MONTEVIDEO

The first species of monkey to be named by auction was called the GoldenPalace.com Monkey in 2005. The monkey was discovered in Madidi National Park.

PARAGUAY

ASUNCIÓN

BOLIVIA

SUCRE

In 1892 fingerprints were used to solve a crime for the first time. Policeman Juan Vucetich proved that prints at a murder scene belonged to the mother of the two victims.

BUENOS AIRES

Necochea

ARGENTINA

Jacinto Aráuz

René Favaloro worked in Jacinto Aráuz before performing the first heart bypass operation in 1967 in Cleveland, Ohio.

National Park

Arequipa

LA PAZ

Nazca **Cusco**

CHILE

Valparaíso

SANTIAGO

Valdivia

The first Nazca lines were created around 200 B.C. The lines form patterns and large images of monkeys, spiders, and other animals that you can only see as a whole from the air.

Byron Rickards became the first aircraft hijack victim in 1931, when his plane was seized at Arequipa by Peruvian revolutionaries.

South America's first submarine made its first test dives in 1866. The pedal-driven sub had two cannons and a crew of 11, who died when the submarine sank in Valparaíso Bay.

Valdivia was named after the first Spanish governor of Chile, Pedro de Valdivia, who founded the city in 1552, 11 years after founding Santiago.

500 miles

500km

0

0

France

France is the biggest country in western Europe. Many famous artists, scientists, explorers, and politicians were born there. The country is known for its rich history, fine food and wine, and its varied landscapes, ranging from the mountainous Alps to rolling farmland to sandy beaches. More vacationers visit France than any other country in the world—more than 80 million people travel there every year.

Nicolas Appert first successfully preserved food at the start of the 1800s. His heat-treated glass jars of peas, beans, and other foods were tested by the French army in Brest.

In 1926 Gertrude Ederle became the first woman to swim across the English Channel. She swam from Gris-Nez, France, to Kingsdown, U.K., in 14½ hours, beating the men's record by almost two hours.

Brest

The first Tour de France began in Paris in 1903 and was won by Maurice Garin. In 2005 American Lance Armstrong *(left)* became the first rider to win the bicycle race seven times.

Filming of the first Indiana Jones movie, *Raiders of the Lost Ark*, began in La Rochelle in 1980. The movie was a hit and took in more than $380 million at the box office.

0   100km

0   100 miles

In 1925 conman Victor Lustig was the first to try to sell the Eiffel Tower. He offered it to scrap metal dealer André Poisson for $100,000.

The first flying trapeze act was performed by Jules Leotard at the Cirque Napoleon in 1859. Leotard also invented the tight-fitting costume worn by gymnasts.

The world's first car service station was opened in 1895 in Bordeaux by Monsieur Borol, who offered gas, repairs, and a place to park.

La Rochelle

Eiffel Tower

River Seine

Place de l'Hotel de Ville

Cirque Napoleon

Pauillac

Bordeau

Bay of Arcachon

PARIS

The first victim of the guillotine invented by Dr. Ignace Guillotin *(right)* was highwayman Nicolas Jacques Peletier, who was executed in 1792.

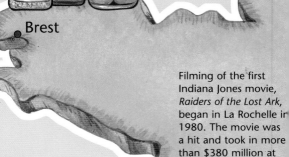

The world's first horror movie was just two minutes long. *Le Manoir du Diable (The Devil's Castle)* was made by Georges Méliès in 1896.

The Dune of Pilat is Europe's biggest sand formation. The gigantic dune is 344 ft. (105m) high, 1,640 ft. (500m) wide and 8,858 ft. (2,700m) long.

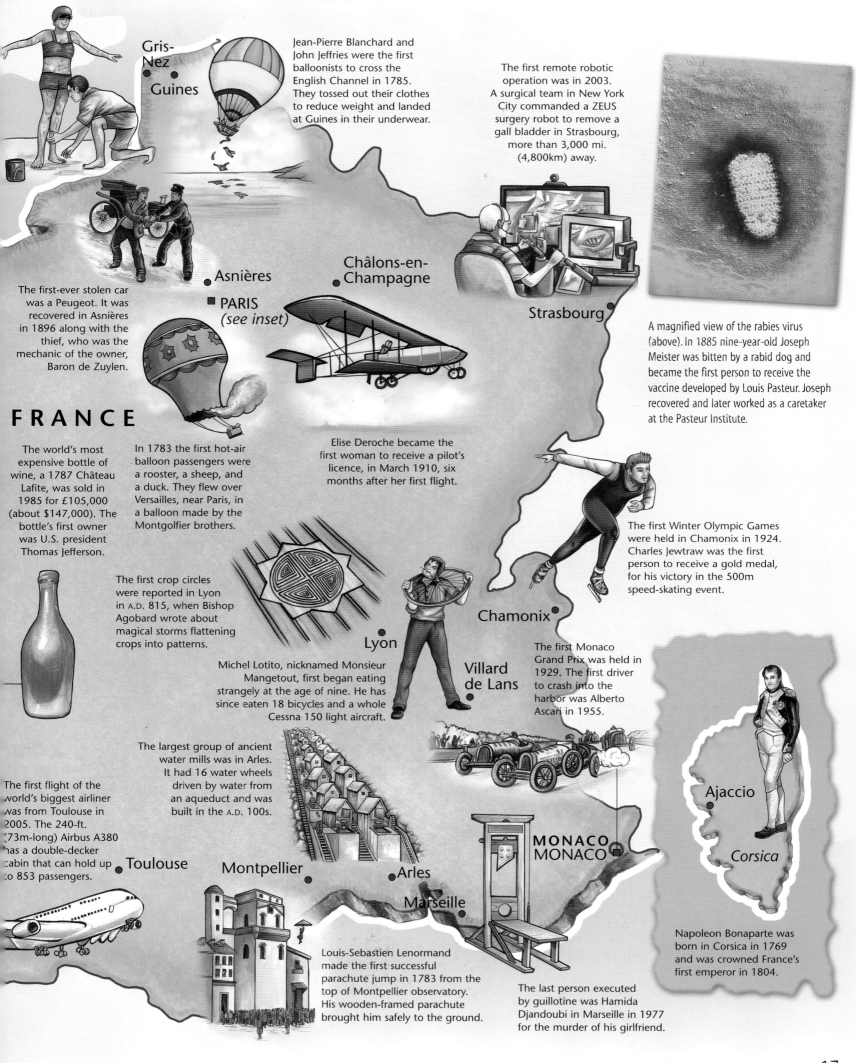

Jean-Pierre Blanchard and John Jeffries were the first balloonists to cross the English Channel in 1785. They tossed out their clothes to reduce weight and landed at Guines in their underwear.

Gris-Nez
Guines

The first remote robotic operation was in 2003. A surgical team in New York City commanded a ZEUS surgery robot to remove a gall bladder in Strasbourg, more than 3,000 mi. (4,800km) away.

Asnières
PARIS
(see inset)
Châlons-en-Champagne
Strasbourg

The first-ever stolen car was a Peugeot. It was recovered in Asnières in 1896 along with the thief, who was the mechanic of the owner, Baron de Zuylen.

A magnified view of the rabies virus (above). In 1885 nine-year-old Joseph Meister was bitten by a rabid dog and became the first person to receive the vaccine developed by Louis Pasteur. Joseph recovered and later worked as a caretaker at the Pasteur Institute.

F R A N C E

The world's most expensive bottle of wine, a 1787 Château Lafite, was sold in 1985 for £105,000 (about $147,000). The bottle's first owner was U.S. president Thomas Jefferson.

In 1783 the first hot-air balloon passengers were a rooster, a sheep, and a duck. They flew over Versailles, near Paris, in a balloon made by the Montgolfier brothers.

Elise Deroche became the first woman to receive a pilot's licence, in March 1910, six months after her first flight.

The first Winter Olympic Games were held in Chamonix in 1924. Charles Jewtraw was the first person to receive a gold medal, for his victory in the 500m speed-skating event.

The first crop circles were reported in Lyon in A.D. 815, when Bishop Agobard wrote about magical storms flattening crops into patterns.

Lyon
Chamonix

Michel Lotito, nicknamed Monsieur Mangetout, first began eating strangely at the age of nine. He has since eaten 18 bicycles and a whole Cessna 150 light aircraft.

Villard de Lans

The first Monaco Grand Prix was held in 1929. The first driver to crash into the harbor was Alberto Ascari in 1955.

The largest group of ancient water mills was in Arles. It had 16 water wheels driven by water from an aqueduct and was built in the A.D. 100s.

The first flight of the world's biggest airliner was from Toulouse in 2005. The 240-ft. (73m-long) Airbus A380 has a double-decker cabin that can hold up to 853 passengers.

Toulouse
Montpellier
Arles
Marseille
MONACO
MONACO

Ajaccio
Corsica

Napoleon Bonaparte was born in Corsica in 1769 and was crowned France's first emperor in 1804.

Louis-Sebastien Lenormand made the first successful parachute jump in 1783 from the top of Montpellier observatory. His wooden-framed parachute brought him safely to the ground.

The last person executed by guillotine was Hamida Djandoubi in Marseille in 1977 for the murder of his girlfriend.

Germany and the Low Countries

Germany first became a single country in 1871, when many smaller states joined together. In 1945, after World War II, it was divided into East and West Germany, but it became one country again in 1990. Now it is the second most populous country in Europe, after Russia. More than 82 million people live there today.

Dutch scientist Christiaan Huygens was the first to discover Saturn's moon, called Titan, in 1655. The following year he found that Saturn's rings are made up of rocks. Huygens also invented the first pendulum clock.

The first successful test launch of the V2 rocket was at Peenemünde in 1942. The V2 was the world's first ballistic missile.

The world's first jet aircraft, the Heinkel He178, first flew at Marienehe in 1939. It had wooden wings and a top speed of 430 mph (700km/h).

Work on the 96-mi. (155km)-long Berlin Wall began in 1961, dividing Berlin into east and west. People began to tear it down in 1989, a year before East and West Germany reunited.

Filming began at the world's oldest surviving movie studio in 1912. Movies made at Babelsburg Studios include *Metropolis* (right).

The first-ever newsreel was filmed by Birt Acres, inventor of 35mm movie film, in 1895. It showed Kaiser Wilhelm II opening the Kiel Canal at Holtenau.

The first recording the Beatles made was in 1962 in Hamburg. They backed singer Tony Sheridan.

In 2008 Bremen was the first German state to set a speed limit on motorways of 75 mph (120km/h). In other parts of Germany there is no speed limit.

The first school for guide dogs was opened in Oldenburg in 1916 by Dr. Gerhard Stalling to help blinded soldiers.

The first flight by the world's oldest surviving airline, KLM, flew from London to Amsterdam Schiphol airport in 1920.

The saxophone, played here by jazz star Branford Marsalis, was invented by the Belgian instrument maker Adolphe Sax in the 1840s. Sax was born in Dinant and first began work on the instrument in his father's workshop in Brussels, before perfecting it in Paris.

The largest flower garden in the world was the idea of the Mayor of Lisse in 1949. Keukenhof is known as the Garden of Europe, and seven million bulbs are planted there every year.

Dutch artist Rembrandt van Rijn opened his first studio in Leiden around 1624. He later moved to Amsterdam, where he painted his most famous works.

Peenemünde

BERLIN
Babelsburg

Marienehe

Holtenau

Hamburg

Bremen

120

Oldenburg

GERMANY

AMSTERDAM
Lisse
Leiden

NETHERLANDS

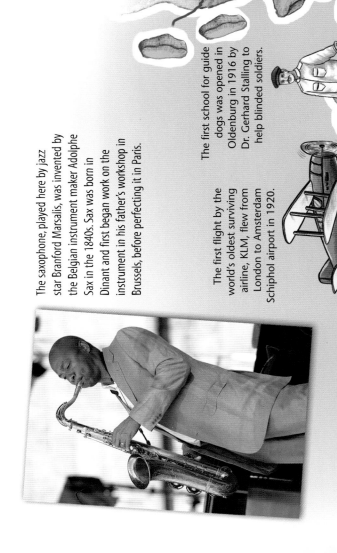

Doberman pinschers were first bred in 1890 by Karl Friedrich Louis Dobermann. He worked in Apolda as a tax collector and bred the dogs to protect him.

The first known disability vehicle was used by Stephen Farfler of Nuremberg around 1650. It was a chair fitted to tricycle wheels moved by hand.

The first official mascot at an Olympic Games was Waldi, a colorful dachshund, at the 1972 games in Munich.

Watercress was first grown in beds as a salad crop by Nicholas Messinger in Erfurt around 1550.

The first fire engine was a wheeled carriage with a lever-operated water pump, designed by a goldsmith, Anthony Blatner, for the town of Augsburg in 1518.

The first Winter Olympian to compete with a broken arm in a cast was Canada's Diana Gordon-Lennox. She skied the combined downhill and slalom event with just one pole at the 1936 games at Garmisch-Partenkirchen.

Wilhelm, published their first book of fairy tales in 1812 while working in Kassel.

• Apolda

Erfurt •

Kassel •

Nuremberg •

• Augsburg

Munich •

Garmisch-Partenkirchen

The first German expressway was opened in 1932 between Cologne and Bonn. It had no speed limit.

Johannes Gutenberg printed the first Bible using movable type in Mainz between 1450 and 1455. He produced about 180 copies.

The world's first airline, DELAG, was formed in 1909 and flew zeppelin airships from 1910. An early destination was the city of Baden-Baden.

of war at the Olympics was in 1920 in Antwerp. The City of London Police Force won, so they remain the reigning Olympic champions.

Mainz •

Baden-Baden •

Ludwig von Bersuda first thought of the sport of underwater rugby in 1961. The first tournament was held at a swimming pool in Müellheim in 1965.

The first and only painting Vincent van Gogh sold in his lifetime was The Red Vineyard in 1890. It was bought in Brussels by painter Anna Boch.

Cologne •
Bonn •

Müellheim •

BELGIUM

LUXEMBOURG

■ BRUSSELS

Huy •

Echternach •

LUXEMBOURG ■

— LUXEMBOURG

Antwerp •

Luxembourg's first and only saint, Saint Willibrord, built an abbey in A.D. 698 at Echternach, Luxembourg's oldest surviving town.

Huy-born instrument maker Jean-Joseph Merlin first demonstrated roller skates in 1760. At a ball in London he skated while playing a violin, but he crashed into an expensive full-length mirror.

100km

100 miles

0

0

The first extreme ironing world championships were held in Munich in 2002. Eighty competitors tried to iron clothes in unusual places, such as on rocks, in water, and even upside down.

19

United Kingdom and Ireland

The United Kingdom has been home to many world-famous writers, scientists, and musicians, from William Shakespeare and Charles Dickens to Isaac Newton and The Beatles. There are four countries in the United Kingdom—England, Scotland, Wales, and Northern Ireland. The Republic of Ireland became independent from Britain in 1922.

The first Beatles album was recorded at London's EMI Studios in 1963 for just £400 (about $560). The studio changed its name to Abbey Road in 1970, a year after the Beatles' album of the same name was recorded there.

Amelia Earhart was the first woman to fly solo across the Atlantic Ocean, landing in fields near Culmore in 1932 after a flight of 14 hours and 56 minutes.

Household electricity first came to the tiny Scottish island of Eigg in 2008. It is generated by wind turbines, solar panels, and hydroelectric power.

Golf's first major competition, the Open Championship, was first played over 36 holes at the Prestwick Golf Club in 1860.

The last major battle to be fought on the British mainland was the 1746 Battle of Culloden. King George II's armies defeated the Scots led by Charles Edward Stuart (Bonnie Prince Charlie).

Robert the Bruce was first crowned King of Scotland at Scone in 1306. He was deposed by the English just afterward but won a historic victory at the Battle of Bannockburn in 1314.

David Beckham's first goal in professional league soccer was scored not for Manchester United but for Preston North End against Doncaster Rovers in 1995, when he was out on loan.

The first Viking raid on England was in A.D. 793. Vikings from Norway attacked the monastery at Lindesfarne, looted its valuables, and killed or captured many monks.

The first cloned mammal was a sheep born in 1997 and known as 6LL3 or Dolly. Dolly lived for six years.

The first public railroad was the Stockton and Darlington, which opened in 1825, when George Stephenson's engine *Locomotion No.1* hauled 600 passengers.

SCOTLAND

Culloden

Scone

Edinburgh

Lindesfarne

Prestwick

Eigg

0   100km
0   100 miles

20

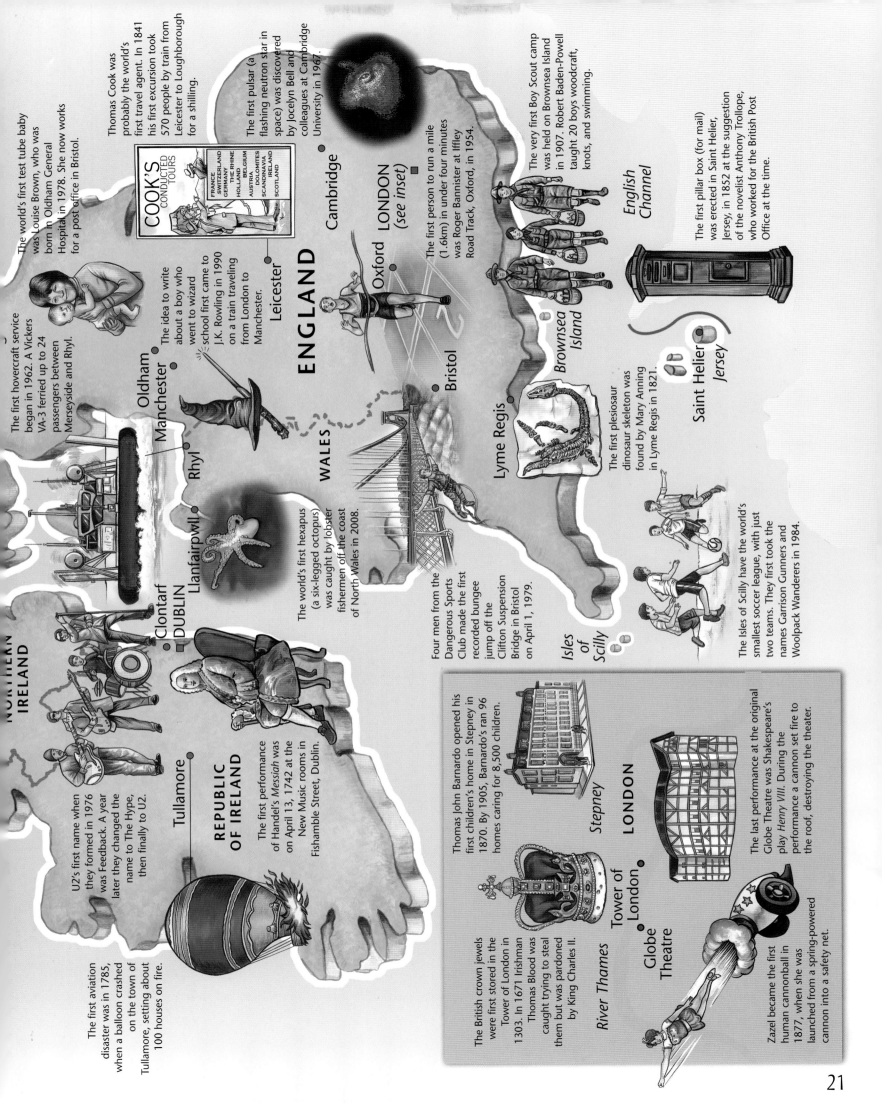

The world's first test tube baby was Louise Brown, who was born in Oldham General Hospital in 1978. She now works for a post office in Bristol.

Thomas Cook was probably the world's first travel agent. In 1841 his first excursion took 570 people by train from Leicester to Loughborough for a shilling.

The first pulsar (a flashing neutron star in space) was discovered by Jocelyn Bell and colleagues at Cambridge University in 1967.

COOK'S CONDUCTED TOURS
FRANCE
SWITZERLAND
GERMANY THE RHINE
HOLLAND BELGIUM
AUSTRALASIA
DOLOMITES
SCANDINAVIA IRELAND
SCOTLAND

Cambridge

LONDON (see inset)

Oxford

ENGLAND

Leicester

The first person to run a mile (1.6km) in under four minutes was Roger Bannister at Iffley Road Track, Oxford, in 1954.

The very first Boy Scout camp was held on Brownsea Island in 1907. Robert Baden-Powell taught 20 boys woodcraft, knots, and swimming.

English Channel

The first pillar box (for mail) was erected in Saint Helier, Jersey, in 1852 at the suggestion of the novelist Anthony Trollope, who worked for the British Post Office at the time.

The first hovercraft service began in 1962. A Vickers VA-3 ferried up to 24 passengers between Merseyside and Rhyl.

The idea to write about a boy who went to wizard school first came to J.K. Rowling in 1990 on a train traveling from London to Manchester.

Oldham
Manchester

Brownsea Island

Bristol

Rhyl

Llanfairpwll

WALES

The world's first hexapus (a six-legged octopus) was caught by lobster fishermen off the coast of North Wales in 2008.

Four men from the Dangerous Sports Club made the first recorded bungee jump off the Clifton Suspension Bridge in Bristol on April 1, 1979.

Lyme Regis

The first plesiosaur dinosaur skeleton was found by Mary Anning in Lyme Regis in 1821.

Saint Helier
Jersey

Clontarf
DUBLIN

Isles of Scilly

The Isles of Scilly have the world's smallest soccer league, with just two teams. They first took the names Garrison Gunners and Woolpack Wanderers in 1984.

NORTHERN IRELAND

U2's first name when they formed in 1976 was Feedback. A year later they changed the name to The Hype, then finally to U2.

Tullamore

REPUBLIC OF IRELAND

The first performance of Handel's *Messiah* was on April 13, 1742 at the New Music rooms in Fishamble Street, Dublin.

The first aviation disaster was in 1785, when a balloon crashed on the town of Tullamore, setting about 100 houses on fire.

Thomas John Barnardo opened his first children's home in Stepney in 1870. By 1905, Barnardo's ran 96 homes caring for 8,500 children.

Stepney

LONDON

The last performance at the original Globe Theatre was Shakespeare's play *Henry VIII*. During the performance a cannon set fire to the roof, destroying the theater.

Tower of London

River Thames

Globe Theatre

The British crown jewels were first stored in the Tower of London in 1303. In 1671 Irishman Thomas Blood was caught trying to steal them but was pardoned by King Charles II.

Zazel became the first human cannonball in 1877, when she was launched from a spring-powered cannon into a safety net.

21

Scandinavia

Scandinavia is the name given to the region of Europe that contains Norway, Sweden, and Denmark. Finland and Iceland are often grouped with them because of their historical and cultural connections. The countries have a long history and many notable firsts. Finland, for example, was the first country in the world to elect female members of parliament, in 1907.

SVALBARD

● Longyearbyen

The Svalbard Global Seed Vault opened at Longyearbyen in 2008, deep inside a mountain. It can hold up to 4.5 million seeds.

Hammerfest was the first town in northern Europe to have electrical street lighting, in 1891.

● Hammerfest

The heavy metal band Lordi filmed their first video in Tornio. In 2006 they won the Eurovision Song Contest with a record score of 292 points.

In 1996 Oikku Ylinen was the first winner of the Air Guitar World Championshin

A post office near Rovaniemi is the first place a letter addressed to Santa Claus is usually sent.

● Rovaniemi

Tornio

Oulu

● Jukkasjärvi

The world's first ice hotel opened in 1990 near Jukkasjärvi. Made of ice blocks from the Torne River, the 80-room hotel is there for just five months every year. Each winter it is rebuilt from scratch.

○ Tromsø

The Our Lady church in Tromsø has the world's most northerly Roman Catholic bishop.

● Bodo

The first Grandmothers' Festival was held at Bodo in 1992. At the first event, Elida Anderson became the world's oldest bungee jumper, aged 79.

ICELAND

■ REYKJAVIK

Iceland's first known settler was Ingólfur Arnarson, who built his home at Reykjavik around A.D. 874.

The island of Surtsey, created by a volcanic eruption on the seabed, was first sighted on November 14, 1963.

○ Surtsey

Norway's first dinosaur find was also the world's deepest. The bone of a Plateosaurus was found in the Snorre offshore oilfield in 2006, 7,402 ft. (2,256m) below the seabed.

Snorre oil field

| 0 | 100km |
| 0 | 100 miles |

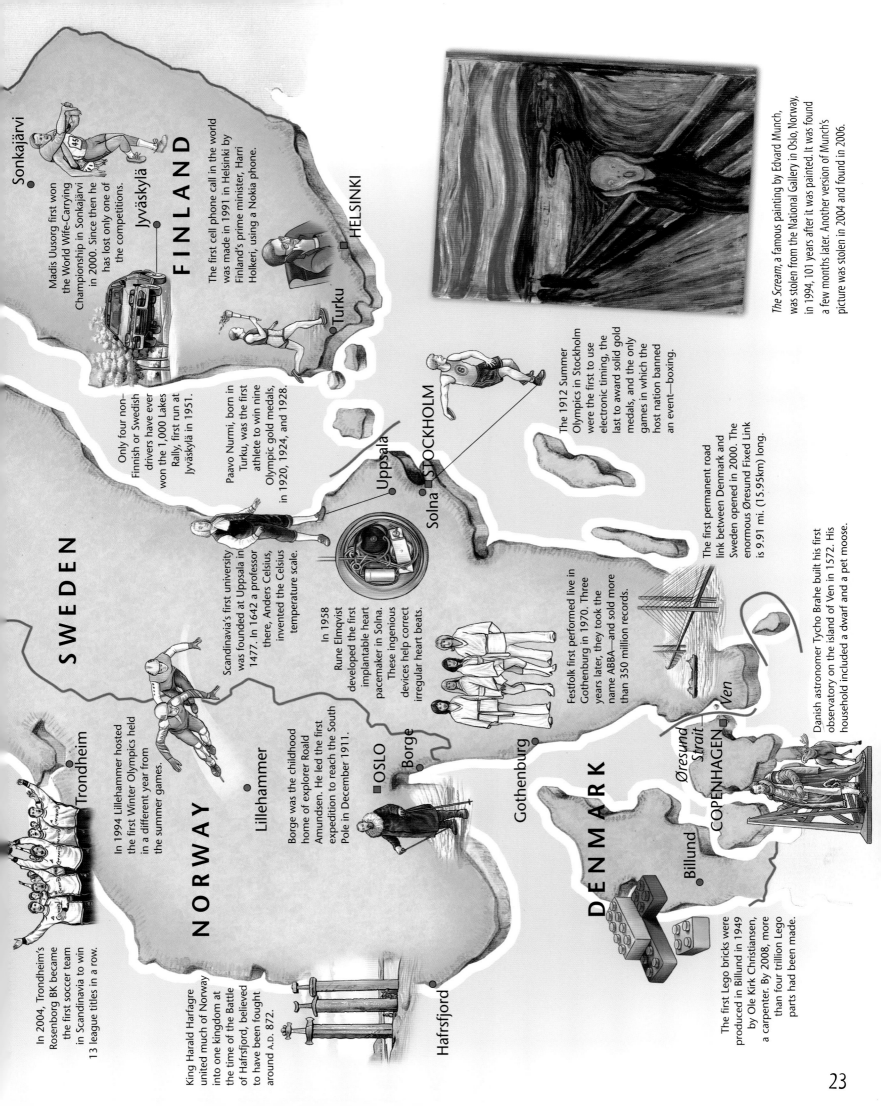

FINLAND

Madis Uusorg first won the World Wife-Carrying Championship in Sonkajärvi in 2000. Since then he has lost only one of the competitions.

Sonkajärvi

Jyväskylä

The first cell phone call in the world was made in 1991 in Helsinki by Finland's prime minister, Harri Holkeri, using a Nokia phone.

HELSINKI

Turku

Only four non–Finnish or Swedish drivers have ever won the 1,000 Lakes Rally, first run at Jyväskylä in 1951.

Paavo Nurmi, born in Turku, was the first athlete to win nine Olympic gold medals, in 1920, 1924, and 1928.

SWEDEN

Uppsala

STOCKHOLM

Solna

The 1912 Summer Olympics in Stockholm were the first to use electronic timing, the last to award solid gold medals, and the only games in which the host nation banned an event—boxing.

Scandinavia's first university was founded at Uppsala in 1477. In 1642 a professor there, Anders Celsius, invented the Celsius temperature scale.

In 1958 Rune Elmqvist developed the first implantable heart pacemaker in Solna. These ingenious devices help correct irregular heart beats.

The first permanent road link between Denmark and Sweden opened in 2000. The enormous Øresund Fixed Link is 9.91 mi. (15.95km) long.

Festfolk first performed live in Gothenburg in 1970. Three years later, they took the name ABBA—and sold more than 350 million records.

Gothenburg

Trondheim

In 2004, Trondheim's Rosenborg BK became the first soccer team in Scandinavia to win 13 league titles in a row.

In 1994 Lillehammer hosted the first Winter Olympics held in a different year from the summer games.

Lillehammer

NORWAY

Borge was the childhood home of explorer Roald Amundsen. He led the first expedition to reach the South Pole in December 1911.

OSLO

Borge

King Harald Harfagre united much of Norway into one kingdom at the time of the Battle of Hafrsfjord, believed to have been fought around A.D. 872.

Hafrsfjord

DENMARK

Billund

COPENHAGEN

Øresund Strait

Ven

Danish astronomer Tycho Brahe built his first observatory on the island of Ven in 1572. His household included a dwarf and a pet moose.

The first Lego bricks were produced in Billund in 1949 by Ole Kirk Christiansen, a carpenter. By 2008, more than four trillion Lego parts had been made.

The Scream, a famous painting by Edvard Munch, was stolen from the National Gallery in Oslo, Norway, in 1994, 101 years after it was painted. It was found a few months later. Another version of Munch's picture was stolen in 2004 and found in 2006.

Spain and Portugal

Spain and Portugal have long coastlines, and many of the world's greatest explorers came from these countries. They both carved out large empires in the Americas, Africa, and Asia. The two countries, together with Andorra, are in a part of southern Europe called the Iberian peninsula, which millions of vacationers visit every year.

The world's first commercial wave farm opened in 2006. The Aguçadora Wave Park near Póvoa de Varzim generates electricity from the movement of ocean waves.

Madeira

Funchal

The first team that soccer player Cristiano Ronaldo played for was CF Andorhina, at the age of eight. He became Manchester United's first Portuguese player in 2003.

Póvoa de Varzim

Porto

Sao Joao is one of the oldest street festivals in Europe. People show their affection by hitting each other on the head gently with plastic hammers!

The first city in the Canaries was Betancuria in 1404. It was named after French explorer Jean de Béthencourt.

La Palma

Santa Cruz

Canary Islands

Betancuria

Europe's longest bridge was opened to traffic in 1998. The Vasco da Gama Bridge measures 10.7 mi. (17.2km) in length.

PORTUGAL

The Spanish Inquisition tried to convert non-Christians and punished those who refused to convert. The first burning at the stake by the inquisition was in 1481 in Seville.

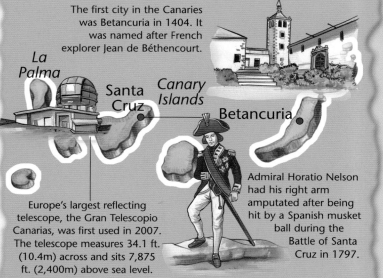

Europe's largest reflecting telescope, the Gran Telescopio Canarias, was first used in 2007. The telescope measures 34.1 ft. (10.4m) across and sits 7,875 ft. (2,400m) above sea level.

Admiral Horatio Nelson had his right arm amputated after being hit by a Spanish musket ball during the Battle of Santa Cruz in 1797.

LISBON

The working title for the Beatles song "Yesterday" was "Scrambled Eggs." Paul McCartney wrote the lyrics while on vacation in the Algarve in 1965.

Portugal's first explorers were funded by Henry the Navigator, based near Sagres. These sailors discovered the Azores in 1427 and sailed farther south down the coast of Africa than any Europeans had before.

The first career of singer Julio Iglesias was as goalie for the Spanish team Real Madrid, which won the first-ever European Cup (now Champions League) in 1956.

Algarve

Palos

Seville

Sagres

Christopher Columbus first set sail across the Atlantic Ocean for the Americas from Palos on August 3, 1492.

Cádiz

The carved face of a creature that is half-cat, half-human was the first religious shrine discovered by archaeologists. The shrine was found in El Juyo cave in 1978 and is about 14,000 years old.

Andorra was first granted a charter by Charlemagne 1,300 years ago. The 70,000 people who live there have the highest life expectancy in the world—83.5 years.

Surrealist painter Salvador Dalí first returned to Figueres, his hometown, after being expelled from Madrid's San Fernando School of Fine Arts in 1926.

 El Juyo

Altamira

ANDORRA

Prehistoric cave paintings were found at Altamira in 1879. There are around 930 paintings in the cave, many showing scenes of bison hunting.

SPAIN

Figueres ●

The first flight by an autogyro (an aircraft with rotors turned by an engine) was made in 1923 in a C4 craft invented by Juan de la Cierva.

Spain's first high-speed train linking Madrid and Barcelona ran in 2008. The AVE trains can reach maximum speeds of 186 mph (300km/h).

Work began on Antoni Gaudi's Sagrada Familia church in 1882. The elaborate 18-tower masterpiece is scheduled to be finished in 2026.

Barcelona ●

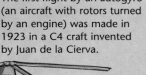

■ MADRID
Cuatro Vientos airfield

Toledo ●

Paella is a traditional Spanish rice dish. The world's largest paella was created in Valencia by Juan Carlos Galbis in 1992. It measured 65.6 ft. (20m) across.

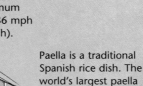

Painter El Greco was born in Crete. In 1577 he moved to Toledo, where he died 37 years later. Many of his most famous paintings were produced there.

Abraham Cresques and his son Jehuda created one of the first atlases in Palma in 1375. Their *Catalan Atlas* is one of the finest examples of medieval mapmaking.

Palma de Majorca

Valencia ●

Buñol ●

The first tomato fight in Buñol happened in 1944. La Tomatina has since become a major event as tourists join locals in hurling 110,200 lbs. (50,000kg) of tomatoes around in a food fight.

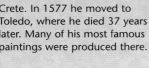

Ibiza

Begun in 784 B.C., the Mezquita is the most magnificent of the 1,000 Muslim mosques in Cordoba. It has more than 1,000 marble, jade, onyx, and granite columns.

The world's biggest nightclub is Privilege in Ibiza, which first opened as a restaurant in the 1970s. It can hold as many as 10,000 dancers.

Cordoba ●

Cartagena

Marbella was a fishing village when a car carrying two rich men broke down there in the 1940s. One of the men built Marbella's first luxury hotel, Hotel Marbella Club, popular with the superrich.

arbella

In 218 B.C. Hannibal traveled north from Cartagena to invade Italy with an army of about 59,000 soldiers and 37 elephants. He ferried the elephants across rivers with rafts.

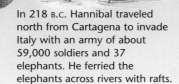

In the first match held at Camp Nou stadium in Barcelona in 1957, the home team beat Legia Warsaw 4–2. Camp Nou is Europe's largest sports stadium and can hold 98,700 people. Michael Jackson, Frank Sinatra, and Bruce Springsteen have played concerts there, and Pope Paul II held a mass at the stadium in 1982.

Cádiz is one of the oldest surviving cities in western Europe. It was also the birthplace of the famous dancer and singer Lola Flores.

The Alpine States and Italy

The Alpine States are named after the Alps, Europe's largest mountain range, which runs through them. Mont Blanc is the highest of the Alps, at 15,774 ft. (4,808m). The region's newest country is Slovenia, which became independent in 1992, and Italy is the largest. Italy includes the two largest islands in the Mediterranean Sea: Sicily and Sardinia.

Georges de Mestral from Lausanne first thought of Velcro in 1941, when he found his dog covered in burrs (seeds with tiny hooks). Fourteen years later, he patented Velcro, made from hundreds of tiny hooks and loops.

Saint Bernard dogs are named after the Saint Bernard monastery high in the Swiss Alps, founded 1,000 years ago.

Ascanio Sobrero discovered the powerful explosive nitroglycerin in 1847 while studying with Théophile-Jules Pelouze at the University of Turin.

The first person to bicycle deep underwater was Italian Vittorio Innocente in 2005. He pedaled his mountain bike more than 164 ft. (50m) at a depth of 197 ft. (60m).

The first April fool hoax on TV was shown on the British program *Panorama* in 1957. A Swiss family in Ticino appeared to harvest spaghetti from trees.

Vaduz, the capital of Liechtenstein, has the smallest stamp museum in the world. The one-room museum is next door to the tourist office.

The oldest natural human mummy in Europe is Otzi the Ice Man. He is about 5,300 years old and was found in the Schnalstal glacier in 1991.

Wolfgang Amadeus Mozart composed his first piece of music on the piano at the age of five.

The colorfully clad Swiss Guard first provided security at Vatican City in 1505. The 100 guards are all unmarried Swiss men between ages 19 and 30.

The very first edition of the communist newspaper *Pravda* was published in Vienna by Leon Trotsky in 1908.

In 1964 Arnold Schwarzenegger started bodybuilding in Graz at the age of 14. Six years later, he won his first Mr. Universe title.

The longest continuous unicycle ride without the feet touching the ground began at Murska Sobota. Joze Voros covered 89.14 mi. (143.46km) in October 2004.

The world's oldest playable musical instrument was found in Divje Babe in 1996. It was made by boring holes into the leg bone of a bear and is 43,000 years old.

Antonio Stradivari settled in Cremona in 1680 and began producing his world-famous violins. More than 600 of his instruments have survived.

Gondolas are narrow boats that travel along Venice's 150 canals. In 2007 Alexandra Hai became the first female gondolier in Venice.

Enzo Ferrari started the Ferrari car company in Modena in 1929. Its famous red vehicles include the Testarossa and the 250GTO, only 36 of which were built.

The first World Formula One Championship was won at Monza by Giuseppe Farina, who won three of the championship's seven races.

PRAVDA

VIENNA
Graz
Salzburg
Murska Sobota
AUSTRIA
Divje Babe
LJUBLJANA
SLOVENIA
Schnalstal Glacier
Venice
Cremona
Modena
VADUZ
LIECH.
Ticino
Monza
BERN
SWITZERLAND
Hospice de St. Bernard
Turin
Genoa
San Remo
Lausanne

0   100km
0   100 miles

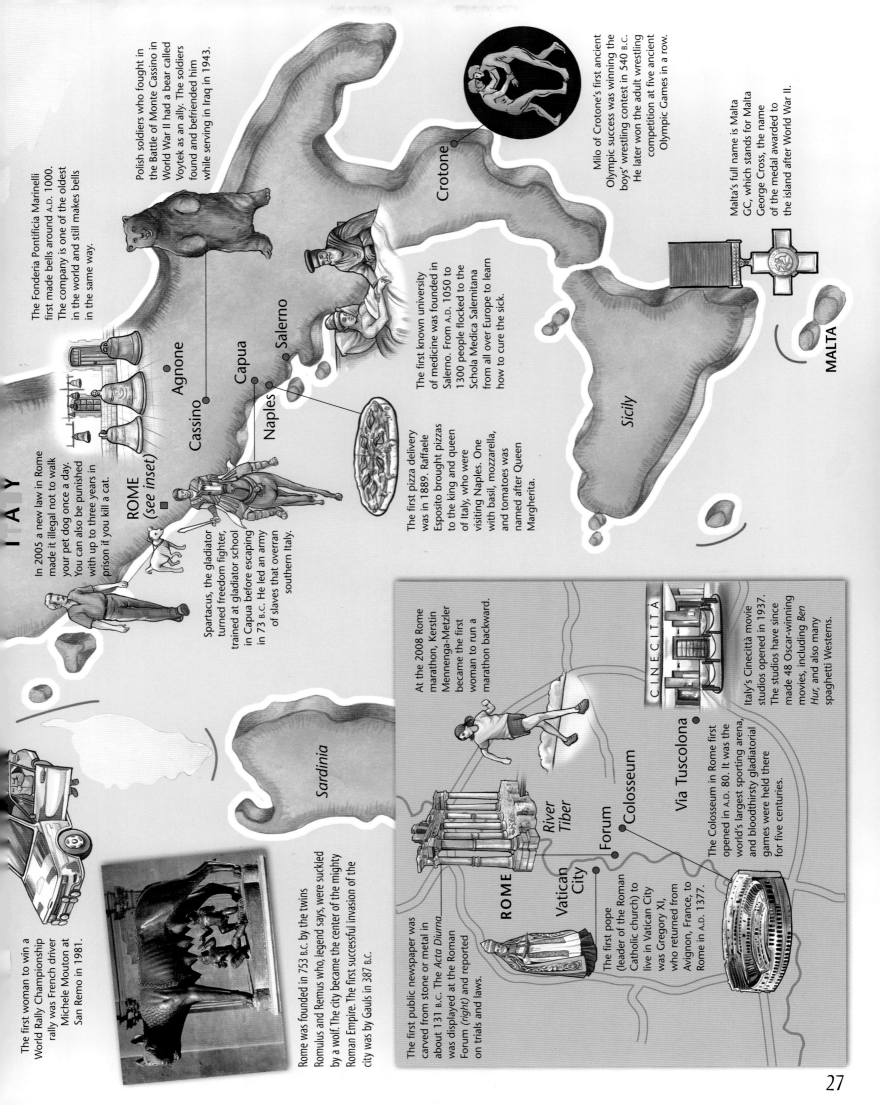

ITALY

The Fonderia Pontificia Marinelli first made bells around A.D. 1000. The company is one of the oldest in the world and still makes bells in the same way.

Polish soldiers who fought in the Battle of Monte Cassino in World War II had a bear called Voytek as an ally. The soldiers found and befriended him while serving in Iraq in 1943.

Milo of Crotone's first ancient Olympic success was winning the boys' wrestling contest in 540 B.C. He later won the adult wrestling competition at five ancient Olympic Games in a row.

Crotone

Malta's full name is Malta GC, which stands for Malta George Cross, the name of the medal awarded to the island after World War II.

MALTA

Agnone

Cassino

Capua

Salerno

Naples

ROME
(see inset)

In 2005 a new law in Rome made it illegal not to walk your pet dog once a day. You can also be punished with up to three years in prison if you kill a cat.

Spartacus, the gladiator turned freedom fighter, trained at gladiator school in Capua before escaping in 73 B.C. He led an army of slaves that overran southern Italy.

The first known university of medicine was founded in Salerno. From A.D. 1050 to 1300 people flocked to the Schola Medica Salernitana from all over Europe to learn how to cure the sick.

The first pizza delivery was in 1889. Raffaele Esposito brought pizzas to the king and queen of Italy, who were visiting Naples. One with basil, mozzarella, and tomatoes was named after Queen Margherita.

Sicily

The first woman to win a World Rally Championship rally was French driver Michele Mouton at San Remo in 1981.

Rome was founded in 753 B.C. by the twins Romulus and Remus who, legend says, were suckled by a wolf. The city became the center of the mighty Roman Empire. The first successful invasion of the city was by Gauls in 387 B.C.

The first public newspaper was carved from stone or metal in about 131 B.C. The *Acta Diurna* was displayed at the Roman Forum *(right)* and reported on trials and laws.

Sardinia

At the 2008 Rome marathon, Kerstin Mennenga-Metzler became the first woman to run a marathon backward.

ROME

River Tiber

Forum

Vatican City

Colosseum

Via Tuscolona

CINECITTÀ

Italy's Cinecittà movie studios opened in 1937. The studios have since made 48 Oscar-winning movies, including *Ben Hur*, and also many spaghetti Westerns.

The Colosseum in Rome first opened in A.D. 80. It was the world's largest sporting arena, and bloodthirsty gladiatorial games were held there for five centuries.

The first pope (leader of the Roman Catholic church) to live in Vatican City was Gregory XI, who returned from Avignon, France, to Rome in A.D. 1377.

Central and eastern Europe

Countries in this part of Europe may once have been part of the Ottoman Empire or the Austro-Hungarian Empire, or, during the 1900s, the Soviet Union. Hungary, Belarus, Moldova, Slovakia, and the Czech Republic are landlocked countries, as they have no coastline. The others either border the Baltic Sea to the north or the Black Sea to the south.

In 2003 Skonto Hall in Riga hosted the Eurovision Song Contest, an annual international competition. It was the first time a Turkish singer, Sertab Erener, won the contest.

TALLINN

ESTONIA

RIGA

LATVIA

Lithuania's first international soccer game ended in a 5–0 defeat by Estonia in 1923. Seventy-two years later, they beat Estonia 7–0 in their biggest-ever international win.

LITHUANIA

Kaunas

RUSSIA

VILNIUS

Frombork

POLAND

The first book to explain that Earth is not at the center of the universe was written by Nicolaus Copernicus in Frombork and published in 1543.

Legendary pole-vaulter Sergei Bubka broke his first world record in Vilnius in 1984, clearing 19.06 ft. (5.81m).

Classical composer and pianist Frederic Chopin was born in Zelazowa Wola in 1810. He was a child prodigy and gave public concerts at the age of seven.

Żelazowa Wola

WARSAW

Łódź

Belavezhskaya Pushcha

Filmmaker Roman Polanski studied at the Polish film school in Lodz. His first full-length film was *Knife in the Water*.

The first (and only) person to survive a fall of more than 32,800 ft. (10,000m) is Yugoslavian air stewardess Vesna Vulovic, when a bomb on her airplane exploded over Srbská Kamenice in 1972!

The first emergency parachute jump ever made was over Warsaw when Jordaki Kurapento's balloon caught fire in 1808.

The Belovezhskaya Pushcha Reserve is an ancient forest that is home to Europe's heaviest wild animal, the European bison. It can weigh 1,980 lbs (900kg) and grow to 7 ft. (2.2m) tall.

Srbská Kamenice

PRAGUE

Wilhelm Steinitz was born in Prague. In 1886 he became the first-ever world chess champion and held the title until 1894.

CZECH REPUBLIC

Vrbové

Móric Benǒvský was born in 1746 in Vrbové. He was an explorer, writer, and soldier who became the first European to be made King of Madagascar, in Africa, in 1776.

SLOVAKIA

BRATISLAVA

The first robot to play chess was The Turk, built by Wolfgang von Kempelen from Bratislava in 1770. In fact, the machine concealed a human chess master inside, but that was not discovered until 1857!

Jászberény

BUDAPEST

HUNGARY

Born in Jászberény, Aladár Gerevich won his first Olympic gold medal for fencing in 1932. Before the 1960 games, he challenged and beat the entire Hungarian saber team to win a place on the Olympic team.

The first ballpoint pen was invented in the 1930s by Budapest-based journalist László József Bíró.

0   100km

0   100 miles

In 1992 Estonia became the first former Soviet republic to issue its own currency, the kroon, from the country's bank in Tallinn.

In 2001 Gintaras Karosas created the world's largest TV sculpture at the Open Air Museum in Vilnius, Lithuania. The sculpture is called *LNK Infotree* and uses 2,903 TV sets covering 10,285 sq. ft. (3,135m²).

The first electric tram in Belarus and much of eastern Europe began running in 1898 in Vitsyebsk.

Vitsyebsk

Orsha

BELARUS

■ MINSK

The first Olympic medal for independent Belarus was won by Igor Zhelezovski, born in Orsha. The speed skater, nicknamed "Igor the Terrible," won a silver medal at the 1994 Winter Olympics.

The first person to appear on Belarus television was news broadcaster Tamara Bastun, on January 1, 1956. The Minsk-based broadcast reached about 4,000 people.

The world's worst nuclear power accident happened at Chernobyl in 1986 when an explosion contaminated thousands of square miles of land with radioactivity. More than 330,000 people were evacuated.

UNICEF

The first Christmas card to benefit charity was published by UNICEF in 1949. It was a painting by seven-year-old Jitka Samkova of Rudolfo, a Czechoslovakian town destroyed during World War II and rebuilt with UNICEF help. Since then, UNICEF has sold more than one billion charity cards.

Chernobyl

■ KIEV

The first U2 spy plane to be shot down was piloted by Francis Gary Powers over Sverdlovsk in 1960. Powers was convicted as an American spy but was released back to the U.S. three years later.

UKRAINE

Oleg Antonov's aircraft design bureau first moved to Ukraine in 1952. Among the Antonov company's aircraft is the gigantic, six-engined AN–225, which is 276 ft. (84m) long.

The Askania-Nova Reserve was first established in 1874 by Fredrich Falz-Fein. It has the largest collection of rare Przewalski's horses in captivity.

Donetsk

Sverdlovsk

MOLDOVA

CHISINAU

Soccer team Sheriff Tiraspol was first formed in 1997 and has made a big impact in Moldovan soccer, winning every league title since 2001.

Tiraspol

Askania-Nova

In 2012 Ukraine will host its first major international sporting event when it holds the Euro2012 soccer championship along with Poland. The Shaktar Donetsk stadium will host five games.

Black Sea

The Crimean War (1853–1856) was the first war in which a correspondent telegraphed reports from the battlefield. William Russell's reports in the British newspaper *The Times* shocked people with the reality of war.

Sevastopol

Southeastern Europe

This region is where the ancient Greek civilization began and where Alexander the Great began his quest to conquer territory as far east as India. Many of the countries were once part of the giant Turkish Ottoman Empire. The region is also known as the Balkans, a name that comes from the Turkish word for chains of wooded mountains.

King Zog 1 was crowned the first king of Albania in 1928. Albania was the first country to change its head of state from a president to a king in the 1900s.

The first flour war in Galaxidi, Greece, probably happened in 1801. Every year people pelt each other with 3,300 lbs. (1,500kg) of flour tinted with food coloring at the start of Lent in the Greek Orthodox religion.

```
0          100km
0          100 miles
```

Nikola Tesla first became fascinated by electricity while studying in Karlovac. He moved to the United States, where his work on electric currents helped to light and power cities.

In 2006 Davor Hundic set a world record for the distance traveled in 24 hours on a jet ski. He started from Icici and covered 641 mi. (1,031km), traveling to Dubrovnik.

King Carol II was born in Sinaia, the first Romanian monarch to be born in the country. He was so interested in soccer that he picked the team for the first soccer World Cup 1930.

Vlad III's reign in Wallachia began in 1456 at his court in Targoviste. He is known as Vlad the Impaler because he impaled his enemies on wooden spikes.

ROMANIA

■ **BUCHAREST**

Petrache Poenaru was born in Craiova but invented the first fountain pen in Paris in 1827. He later designed the

Gabriela Ciucur from Targu Jiu became the first legally registered witch in Romania in 2006.

Sinaia •
Targoviste •

Targu Jiu •
Craiova •

Belgrade was the city that held the first-ever FINA World Swimming Championships in 1973.

BELGRADE ■

Archduke Franz Ferdinand was the heir to the Austro-Hungarian Empire. In 1914 he was assassinated in Sarajevo by Gavrilo Princip. The murder sparked World War I.

CROATIA

**BOSNIA &
HERZEGOVINA**

■ **ZAGREB**
Karlovac •

• Icici

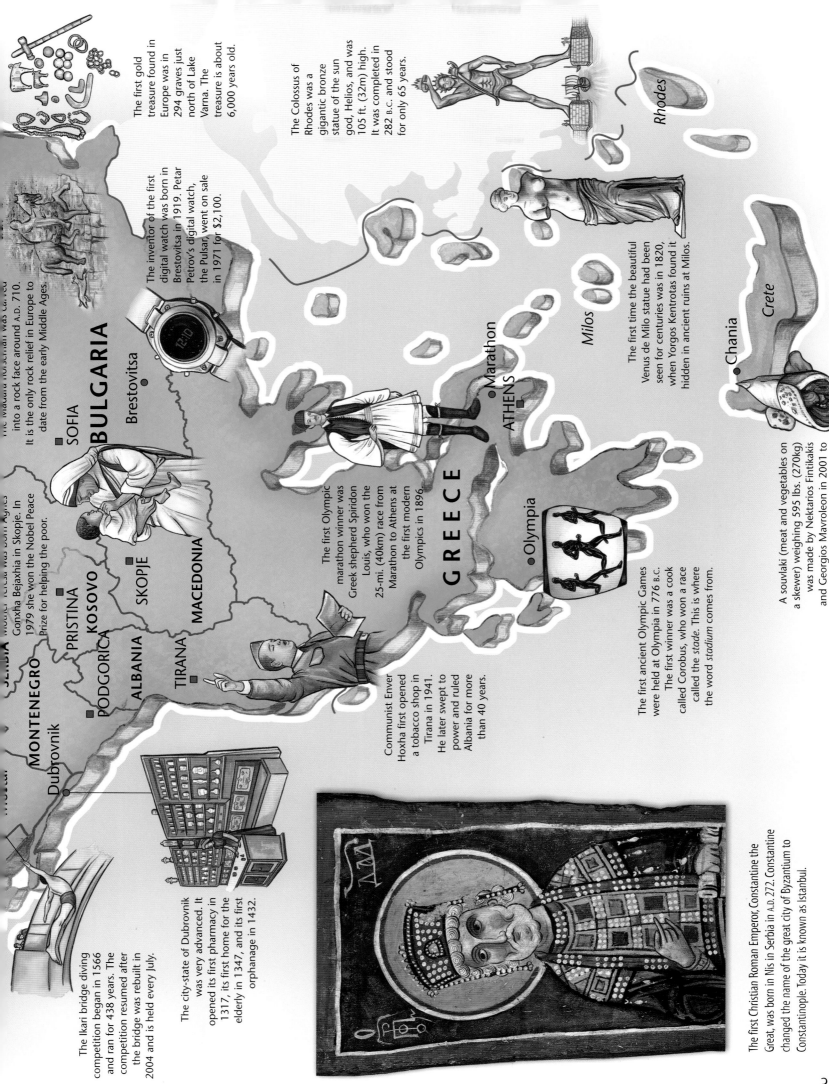

The first gold treasure found in Europe was in 294 graves just north of Lake Varna. The treasure is about 6,000 years old.

The inventor of the first digital watch was born in Brestovitsa in 1919. Petar Petrov's digital watch, the Pulsar, went on sale in 1971 for $2,100.

...into a rock face around A.D. 710. It is the only rock relief in Europe to date from the early Middle Ages.

The Colossus of Rhodes was a gigantic bronze statue of the sun god, Helios, and was 105 ft. (32m) high. It was completed in 282 B.C. and stood for only 65 years.

Rhodes

BULGARIA

SOFIA

Brestovitsa

...Mother Teresa was born Agnes Gonxha Bejaxhia in Skopje. In 1979 she won the Nobel Peace Prize for helping the poor.

MACEDONIA

SKOPJE

PRISTINA

KOSOVO

PODGORICA

ALBANIA

MONTENEGRO

Dubrovnik

TIRANA

The first Olympic marathon winner was Greek shepherd Spiridon Louis, who won the 25-mi. (40km) race from Marathon to Athens at the first modern Olympics in 1896.

Marathon

ATHENS

G R E E C E

Milos

The first time the beautiful Venus de Milo statue had been seen for centuries was in 1820, when Yorgos Kentrotas found it hidden in ancient ruins at Milos.

Chania

Crete

Communist Enver Hoxha first opened a tobacco shop in Tirana in 1941. He later swept to power and ruled Albania for more than 40 years.

Olympia

The first ancient Olympic Games were held at Olympia in 776 B.C. The first winner was a cook called Corobus, who won a race called the *stade*. This is where the word *stadium* comes from.

A souvlaki (meat and vegetables on a skewer) weighing 595 lbs. (270kg) was made by Nektarios Fintikakis and Georgios Mavroleon in 2001 to fill the world's largest pita bread.

The Ikari bridge diving competition began in 1566 and ran for 438 years. The competition resumed after the bridge was rebuilt in 2004 and is held every July.

The city-state of Dubrovnik was very advanced. It opened its first pharmacy in 1317, its first home for the elderly in 1347, and its first orphanage in 1432.

The first Christian Roman Emperor, Constantine the Great, was born in Nis in Serbia in A.D. 272. Constantine changed the name of the great city of Byzantium to Constantinople. Today it is known as Istanbul.

Russia and its neighbors

Russia is the largest country in the world and covers about one-eighth of all the land. The country has the world's second-largest forest, after the Amazon, and Europe's longest river, the Volga. Russia's coastline is more than 23,000 mi. (37,000km) long.

Novaya Zemlya

The first and only time the world's most powerful nuclear weapon was detonated was in 1961 over Novaya Zemlya. The RDS-220 was known as the Tsar Bomba.

RUSSIA

The drilling of the Kola Superdeep Bore Hole began in 1970. The deepest hole was 7.6 mi. (12.3km) deep and reached rocks 2.7 billion years old.

The NS *Lenin* was the world's first nuclear-powered ship. It was built in and launched from St. Petersburg in 1959 and spent 30 years as an icebreaker.

Kola Peninsula

Tomsk State University was the first university in Siberia. It was founded in Tomsk in 1878.

Pyotr Ilyich Tchaikovsky had his first piano lesson at the age of five in Votkinsk. He later became a world-famous composer of ballet music.

Boris Yeltsin was born in Butka. In 1991 he became the first president of Russia to be elected after the breakup of the Soviet Union.

St Petersburg

The popular game Tetris first hit computer screens in 1985. The designer, Alexey Pajitnov, worked at a Moscow computing center.

Butka

Votkinsk

The Baikonur Cosmodrome first opened in 1955. Yuri Gargarin became the first man in space after blasting off from there in 1962.

Tomsk

At the Battle of Talas, near Taraz, in A.D. 751, Arab forces captured Chinese paper makers and brought paper to the Middle East and Europe for the first time.

Obninsk MOSCOW

The 6,000 rock paintings at Gobustan were first found by quarry workers during the 1930s. They also found a stone instrument called a gaval dash.

The first nuclear plant to generate electricity for a power grid started operating in Obninsk in 1954. The reactor produced power for around 2,000 homes.

Baikonur

KAZAKHSTAN

Taraz Almaty

The first commercial service by a supersonic aircraft flew to Almaty. The Soviet Tu-144 began flying mail and freight in December 1975.

GEORGIA

Batumi

UZBEKISTAN

TASHKENT **KYRGYZSTAN**

Gobustan

TURKMENISTAN

AZERBAIJAN

ARMENIA

DUSHANBE **TAJIKISTAN**

The first time Josef Stalin was arrested and sent to Siberia was in Batumi in 1902, for organizing strikes. He later became leader of the Soviet Union.

The Karakum Canal in Turkmenistan is the largest water supply canal in the world, carrying water from the Amu Darya river across the desert.

The Uthman Qur'an is the oldest Qur'an (Muslim holy book) in existence. It was first completed in about 655 B.C. and was brought to Uzbekistan by Tamerlane.

Timur the Lame (Tamerlane) was born in Shahrisabz in 1336. He made Samarkand his capital and invaded Armenia, Georgia, and India. In Isfahan, Iran, he built towers from the skulls of 70,000 enemies. This painting shows his warriors attacking a walled town.

Woolly mammoth remains about 20,000 years old were first discovered by nine-year-old Simion Jarkov near Novorybnoye in 1997.

Novorybnoye

Ivan the Terrible built St. Basil's Cathedral in Moscow to celebrate the capture of Kazan from the Mongols. Legends say that the architect of the cathedral was blinded so that he could not design anything as beautiful again.

nguska River

In 1908 there was an explosion over the Tunguska River that was 1,000 times more powerful than the first atomic bomb. It was probably an exploding comet or meteorite.

Oymyakon

Oymyakon is the world's coldest village, with temperatures as low as –94°F (–70°C). Its 800 inhabitants really have to wrap up warm!

Lake Baikal is the world's deepest lake, at 5,371 ft. (1,637m). It was discovered in 1643 and is so deep that scientists believe it holds one-fifth of the world's fresh water.

Lake Baikal

Drilling began on the Z-11 oil well on Sakhalin Island in 2007 and was completed in 61 days. At 37,014 ft. (11,282m), it is the deepest oil well in the world.

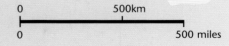

0   500km

0   500 miles

Sakhalin Island

Vladivostok

The construction of the Trans-Siberian Railroad began in 1891. The line is 5,800 mi. (9,300km) long, and the first trains took nine days to travel from Vladivostok to Moscow.

MiG aircraft designer Artem Mikoyan was born in 1905 in Sanahin, Armenia. His first successful jet fighter was the MiG-15, which first flew in 1948. More than 18,000 were eventually built.

Africa

Africa is the second-largest continent in the world and is home to more than 960 million people. The country has the world's largest desert, the Sahara, as well as lush tropical rainforests in its center. Most scientists believe that the ancestors of the first human beings came from Africa.

Ibn Battuta was probably the world's first tourist. He left Tangier in 1325 to make a pilgrimage to Mecca and then visited China, India, Russia, and East Africa during a 30-year trek.

In 1415 Ceuta became Portugal's first colony. It is now part of Spain and has a helicopter service that flies regularly to Malaga.

The world's longest conveyor belt was built in the 1970s. It is 62 mi. (100km) long and carries phosphate from mines in Bu Craa to the coast.

Frenchmen Alain Génestier and Joseph Terbiaut won the first Paris-Dakar rally in 1979, driving a Range Rover.

The first European settlement in West Africa was São Jorge da Mina (or Elmina) in Ghana, founded in 1482. The first trading stations were set up around Elmina by European slave traders.

Filming on the first *Star Wars* movie began in March 1976. Director George Lucas used the desert around Tawzar to represent the planet Tatooine.

A temperature of 136°F (57.8°C) was recorded at El Azizia in Libya on September 13, 1922—the hottest ever measured.

The Richat Structure was first seen from space by the *Gemini IV* mission in 1965. The 31-mi. (50km)-wide basin in the Sahara Desert was probably formed by erosion.

Timbuktu was first settled by Tuareg tribespeople more than 1,000 years ago. Its Islamic university was founded in the 1320s.

The first woman to become the wife of presidents of two different countries was Graca Machel. She was married to President Machel of Mozambique until he died in a plane crash in 1986. She then married Nelson Mandela in Johannesburg in 1998.

Haile Selassie was born near Harer. He was crowned Emperor of Ethiopia in 1930, and in 1954 he became the first head of state to visit West Germany after World War II.

Lake Asal is the lowest point in Africa, 502 ft. (153m) below sea level. It is the world's saltiest lake and has about nine times more salt than seawater.

The first non-Africans to find Lake Chad were Dixon Denham and Hugh Clapperton in 1823. The lake was gigantic—about

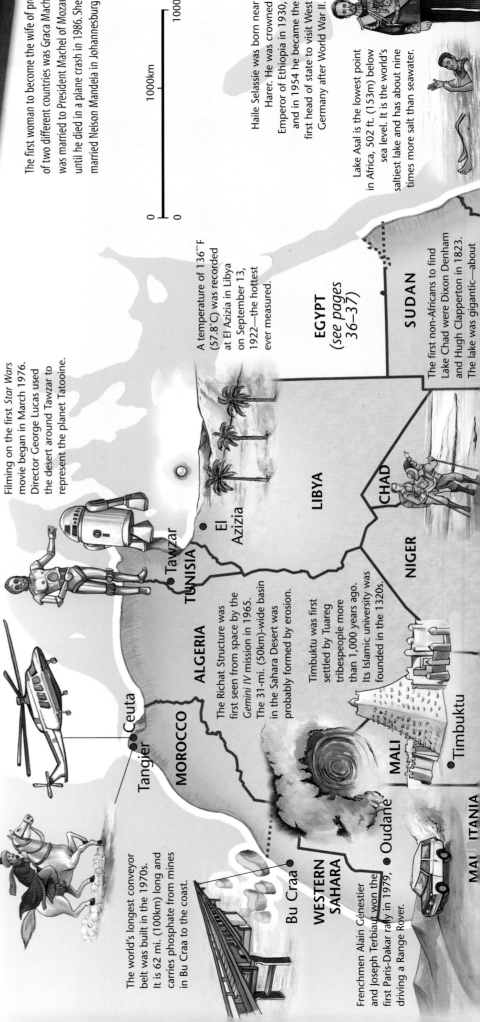

1000km

1000 miles

EGYPT
(see pages 36–37)

SUDAN

LIBYA

CHAD

El Azizia

NIGER

TUNISIA

Tawzar

ALGERIA

MALI

MOROCCO

Ceuta

Tangier

Timbuktu

WESTERN SAHARA

Bu Craa

Oudane

MAURITANIA

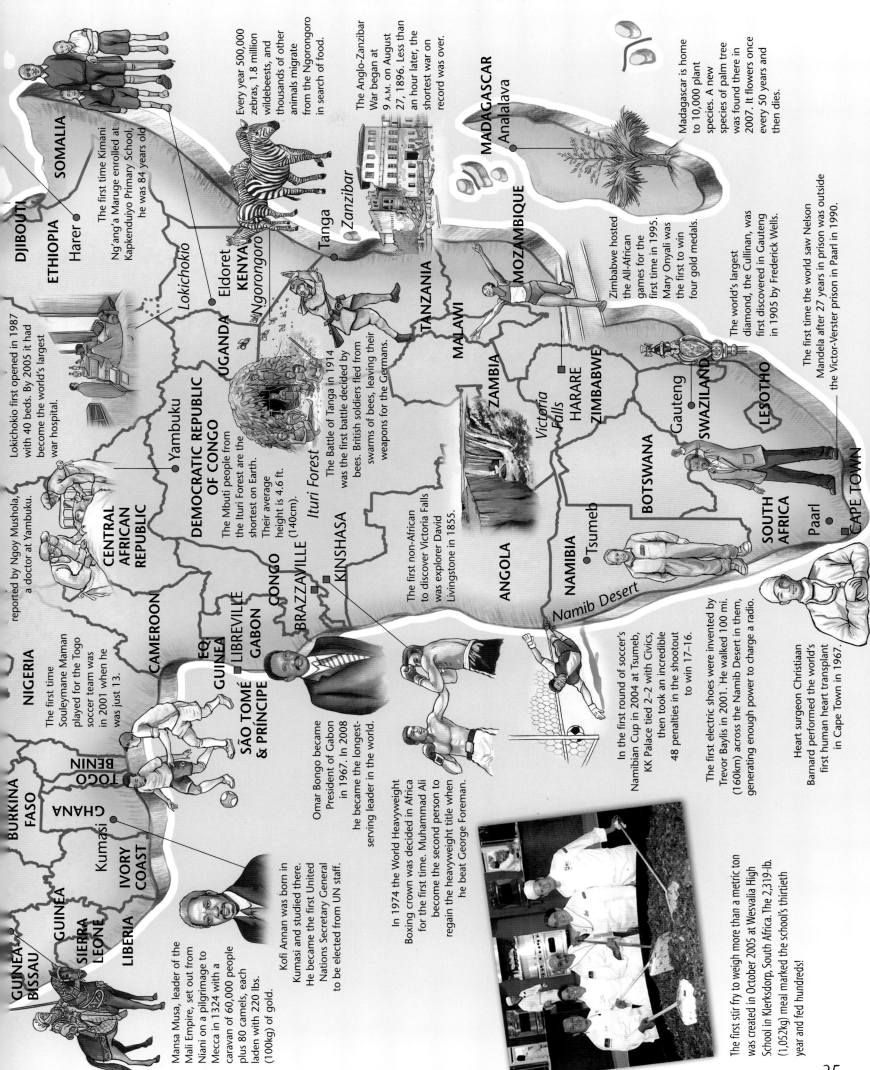

GUINEA-BISSAU

GUINEA

SIERRA LEONE

LIBERIA

IVORY COAST
Kumasi

GHANA

TOGO

BENIN

BURKINA FASO

NIGERIA

CAMEROON

CENTRAL AFRICAN REPUBLIC

EQ. GUINEA

SÃO TOMÉ & PRÍNCIPE

GABON
LIBREVILLE

CONGO
BRAZZAVILLE

DEMOCRATIC REPUBLIC OF CONGO
Yambuku
KINSHASA

UGANDA

KENYA
Eldoret
Lokichokio

ETHIOPIA
Harer

SOMALIA

DJIBOUTI

Ngorongoro

Tanga
Zanzibar

TANZANIA

MALAWI

ZAMBIA
Victoria Falls

MOZAMBIQUE

MADAGASCAR
Analalava

ANGOLA

NAMIBIA
Tsumeb
Namib Desert

BOTSWANA

ZIMBABWE
HARARE

SWAZILAND

LESOTHO

Gauteng

SOUTH AFRICA
Paarl
CAPE TOWN

Ituri Forest

reported by Ngoy Mushola, a doctor at Yambuku.

Mansa Musa, leader of the Mali Empire, set out from Niani on a pilgrimage to Mecca in 1324 with a caravan of 60,000 people plus 80 camels, each laden with 220 lbs. (100kg) of gold.

Kofi Annan was born in Kumasi and studied there. He became the first United Nations Secretary General to be elected from UN staff.

The first time Souleymane Maman played for the Togo soccer team was in 2001 when he was just 13.

In 1974 the World Heavyweight Boxing crown was decided in Africa for the first time. Muhammad Ali become the second person to regain the heavyweight title when he beat George Foreman.

Omar Bongo became President of Gabon in 1967. In 2008 he became the longest-serving leader in the world.

The first non-African to discover Victoria Falls was explorer David Livingstone in 1855.

The Mbuti people from the Ituri Forest are the shortest on Earth. Their average height is 4.6 ft. (140cm).

The Battle of Tanga in 1914 was the first battle decided by bees. British soldiers fled from swarms of bees, leaving their weapons for the Germans.

Lokichokio first opened in 1987 with 40 beds. By 2005 it had become the world's largest war hospital.

The first time Kimani Ng'ang'a Maruge enrolled at Kapkenduiyo Primary School, he was 84 years old

Every year 500,000 zebras, 1.8 million wildebeests, and thousands of other animals migrate from the Ngorongoro in search of food.

The Anglo-Zanzibar War began at 9 A.M. on August 27, 1896. Less than an hour later, the war on record was over.

Madagascar is home to 10,000 plant species. A new species of palm tree was found there in 2007. It flowers once every 50 years and then dies.

Zimbabwe hosted the All-African games for the first time in 1995. Mary Onyali was the first to win four gold medals.

The world's largest diamond, the Cullinan, was first discovered in Gauteng in 1905 by Frederick Wells.

The first time the world saw Nelson Mandela after 27 years in prison was outside the Victor-Verster prison in Paarl in 1990.

The first electric shoes were invented by Trevor Baylis in 2001. He walked 100 mi. (160km) across the Namib Desert in them, generating enough power to charge a radio.

In the first round of soccer's Namibian Cup in 2004 at Tsumeb, KK Palace tied 2–2 with Civics, then took an incredible 48 penalties in the shootout to win 17–16.

Heart surgeon Christiaan Barnard performed the world's first human heart transplant in Cape Town in 1967.

The first stir fry to weigh more than a metric ton was created in October 2005 at Wesvalia High School in Klerksdorp, South Africa. The 2,319-lb. (1,052kg) meal marked the school's thirtieth year and fed hundreds!

Southwest Asia and Egypt

The three continents of Africa, Asia, and Europe meet here. Three of the world's biggest religions —Christianity, Islam, and Judaism—were founded in this region. Much of the land is rocky and mountainous or sandy desert, but there are areas of fertile farmland as well as huge amounts of oil beneath the ground.

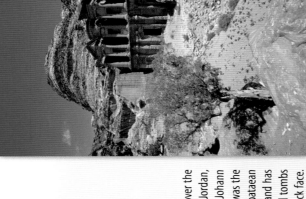

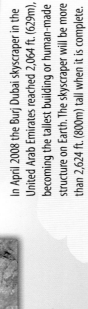

Zildjian cymbals were first made in 1623 in Istanbul. An Armenian alchemist called Avedis found that sheets of his metal alloy made musical sounds when struck.

During the Crusades European Christians invaded Muslim lands. The first city captured by siege was Nicaea (now Iznik) in 1097.

The first person to rediscover the amazing city of Petra, in Jordan, was Swiss explorer Johann Burckhardt in 1812. It was the capital city of the Nabataean Kingdom in the 300s B.C. and has magnificent buildings and tombs carved from the solid rock face.

Al-Jazari was the first engineer to record the moving parts of water clocks at the Artuklu Palace in Diyarbakir. He wrote his *Book of Knowledge of Ingenious Mechanical Devices* in 1206.

Six of the earliest winemaking jars ever found were discovered at Hajji Firuz Tepe. They hold about 2.3 gal. (9l) of wine each and are about 7,000 years old.

In Cyprus in 2004 Thomas Cucchi found the first new mammal in Europe for more than a century. The gray mouse has a larger head and teeth than others.

The 101-mi. (163km)-long Suez Canal opened in 1869, shortening journeys from the Mediterranean to Asia by thousands of miles.

In April 2008 the Burj Dubai skyscraper in the United Arab Emirates reached 2,064 ft. (629m), becoming the tallest building or human-made structure on Earth. The skyscraper will be more than 2,624 ft. (800m) tall when it is complete.

Soccer striker Ali Daei was born in Ardabil and scored his first goal for Iran in 1993. He has scored 109 goals in 149 matches, more than any other male soccer player.

The term *assassin* came from an Islamic order called the Hashshashin that began around 1090. Their headquarters were at a castle called Alamut, which means "death castle."

300km

300 miles

0

0

TURKEY

- Istanbul
- Iznik
- ■ ANKARA
- Diyarbakir

SYRIA

Hajji Firuz Tepe

Ardabil

Gaugamela

Qazvin

■ TEHRAN

IRA

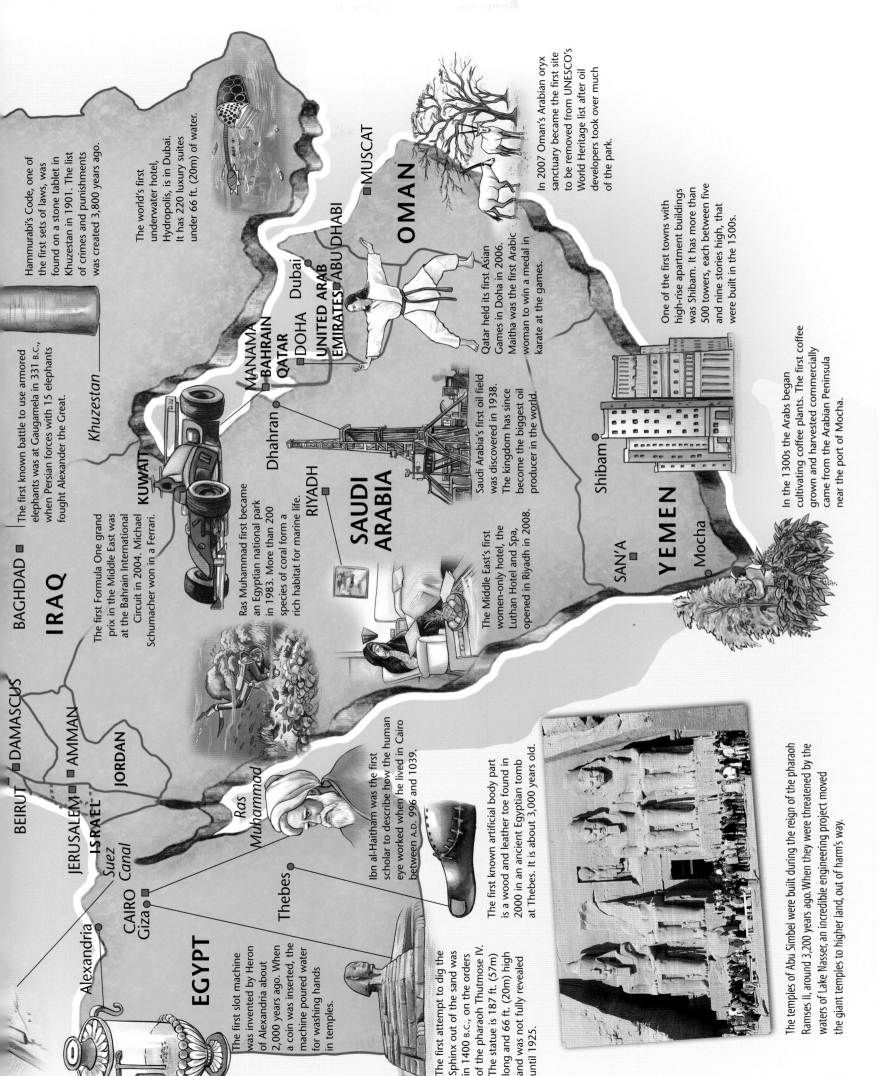

Hammurabi's Code, one of the first sets of laws, was found on a stone tablet in Khuzestan in 1901. The list of crimes and punishments was created 3,800 years ago.

The world's first underwater hotel, Hydropolis, is in Dubai. It has 220 luxury suites under 66 ft. (20m) of water.

IRAQ

BAGHDAD ■

■ DAMASCUS
BEIRUT ■

JERUSALEM ■
ISRAEL
AMMAN ■
JORDAN

Khuzestan

The first known battle to use armored elephants was at Gaugamela in 331 B.C., when Persian forces with 15 elephants fought Alexander the Great.

The first Formula One grand prix in the Middle East was at the Bahrain International Circuit in 2004. Michael Schumacher won in a Ferrari.

KUWAIT

MANAMA
BAHRAIN
QATAR
DOHA ■ Dubai
UNITED ARAB EMIRATES ■ ABU DHABI

■ MUSCAT

OMAN

In 2007 Oman's Arabian oryx sanctuary became the first site to be removed from UNESCO's World Heritage list after oil developers took over much of the park.

Ras Muhammad first became an Egyptian national park in 1983. More than 200 species of coral form a rich habitat for marine life.

Dhahran ●

Saudi Arabia's first oil field was discovered in 1938. The kingdom has since become the biggest oil producer in the world.

Qatar held its first Asian Games in Doha in 2006. Maitha was the first Arabic woman to win a medal in karate at the games.

One of the first towns with high-rise apartment buildings was Shibam. It has more than 500 towers, each between five and nine stories high, that were built in the 1500s.

RIYADH ■

SAUDI ARABIA

The Middle East's first women-only hotel, the Luthan Hotel and Spa, opened in Riyadh in 2008.

Shibam ●

Suez Canal
Alexandria ●
CAIRO ■
Giza ●

Ras Muhammad

Ibn al-Haitham was the first scholar to describe how the human eye worked when he lived in Cairo between A.D. 996 and 1039.

The first known artificial body part is a wood and leather toe found in 2000 in an ancient Egyptian tomb at Thebes. It is about 3,000 years old.

SAN'A ■

YEMEN

Mocha ●

In the 1300s the Arabs began cultivating coffee plants. The first coffee grown and harvested commercially came from the Arabian Peninsula near the port of Mocha.

EGYPT

The first slot machine was invented by Heron of Alexandria about 2,000 years ago. When a coin was inserted, the machine poured water for washing hands in temples.

Thebes ●

The first attempt to dig the Sphinx out of the sand was in 1400 B.C., on the orders of the pharaoh Thutmose IV. The statue is 187 ft. (57m) long and 66 ft. (20m) high and was not fully revealed until 1925.

The temples of Abu Simbel were built during the reign of the pharaoh Ramses II, around 3,200 years ago. When they were threatened by the waters of Lake Nasser, an incredible engineering project moved the giant temples to higher land, out of harm's way.

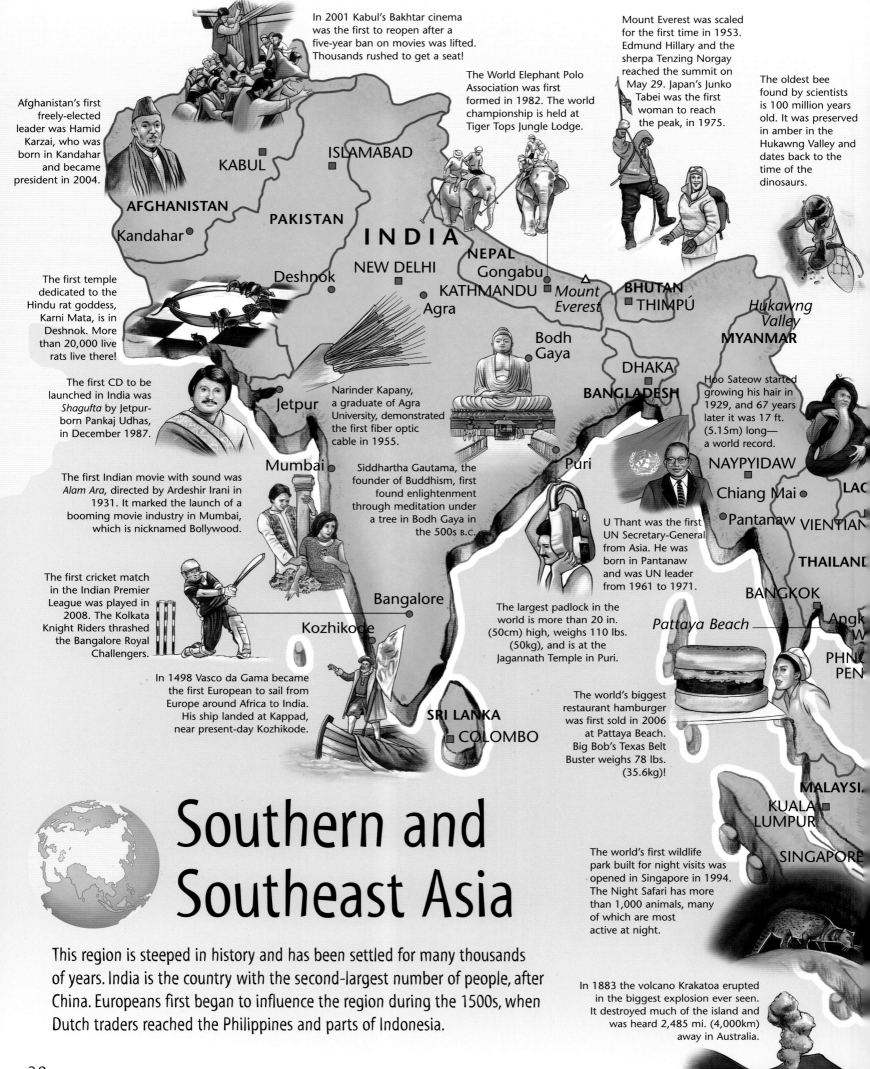

In 2001 Kabul's Bakhtar cinema was the first to reopen after a five-year ban on movies was lifted. Thousands rushed to get a seat!

The World Elephant Polo Association was first formed in 1982. The world championship is held at Tiger Tops Jungle Lodge.

Mount Everest was scaled for the first time in 1953. Edmund Hillary and the sherpa Tenzing Norgay reached the summit on May 29. Japan's Junko Tabei was the first woman to reach the peak, in 1975.

The oldest bee found by scientists is 100 million years old. It was preserved in amber in the Hukawng Valley and dates back to the time of the dinosaurs.

Afghanistan's first freely-elected leader was Hamid Karzai, who was born in Kandahar and became president in 2004.

KABUL
ISLAMABAD
AFGHANISTAN
PAKISTAN
Kandahar
I N D I A
NEPAL
Deshnok
NEW DELHI
Gongabu
KATHMANDU
Mount Everest
BHUTAN
THIMPÚ
Agra
Hukawng Valley
MYANMAR

The first temple dedicated to the Hindu rat goddess, Karni Mata, is in Deshnok. More than 20,000 live rats live there!

Bodh Gaya

The first CD to be launched in India was *Shagufta* by Jetpur-born Pankaj Udhas, in December 1987.

Narinder Kapany, a graduate of Agra University, demonstrated the first fiber optic cable in 1955.

DHAKA
BANGLADESH

Hoo Sateow started growing his hair in 1929, and 67 years later it was 17 ft. (5.15m) long— a world record.

Jetpur

NAYPYIDAW

Mumbai

Siddhartha Gautama, the founder of Buddhism, first found enlightenment through meditation under a tree in Bodh Gaya in the 500s B.C.

Puri

Chiang Mai
LAC
Pantanaw
VIENTIAN

The first Indian movie with sound was *Alam Ara*, directed by Ardeshir Irani in 1931. It marked the launch of a booming movie industry in Mumbai, which is nicknamed Bollywood.

U Thant was the first UN Secretary-General from Asia. He was born in Pantanaw and was UN leader from 1961 to 1971.

THAILAND

BANGKOK

The first cricket match in the Indian Premier League was played in 2008. The Kolkata Knight Riders thrashed the Bangalore Royal Challengers.

Bangalore

Kozhikode

The largest padlock in the world is more than 20 in. (50cm) high, weighs 110 lbs. (50kg), and is at the Jagannath Temple in Puri.

Pattaya Beach
Angk
W
PHN
PEN

In 1498 Vasco da Gama became the first European to sail from Europe around Africa to India. His ship landed at Kappad, near present-day Kozhikode.

SRI LANKA
COLOMBO

The world's biggest restaurant hamburger was first sold in 2006 at Pattaya Beach. Big Bob's Texas Belt Buster weighs 78 lbs. (35.6kg)!

MALAYSI.
KUALA LUMPUR
SINGAPORE

Southern and Southeast Asia

The world's first wildlife park built for night visits was opened in Singapore in 1994. The Night Safari has more than 1,000 animals, many of which are most active at night.

This region is steeped in history and has been settled for many thousands of years. India is the country with the second-largest number of people, after China. Europeans first began to influence the region during the 1500s, when Dutch traders reached the Philippines and parts of Indonesia.

In 1883 the volcano Krakatoa erupted in the biggest explosion ever seen. It destroyed much of the island and was heard 2,485 mi. (4,000km) away in Australia.

Bangkok was given its full name by King Buddha Yodfa Chulaloke, who ruled Thailand between 1782 and 1809. At 167 letters long, it is the longest place name in the world. The full name is Krungthep Maha Nakorn, Amarn Rattanakosindra, Mahindrayudhya, Mahadilokpop Noparatana Rajdhani Mahasathan, Amorn Piman Avatarn Satit, Sakkatultiya Vishnukarn Prasit.

The spectacular Buddhist monument of Borobudur in Indonesia was first rediscovered in 1814 by Dutch engineer H. C. Cornelius. It was built around A.D. 800 and has nine levels and more than 500 statues of Buddha. It was abandoned several centuries later and then buried in volcanic ash and rainforest plants.

VIETNAM

HANOI

In 2000 Tran Hieu Ngan from Tuy Hoa won Vietnam's first-ever Olympic medal, a silver in the women's tae kwon do competition.

PHILIPPINES

MANILA

Lubang Island

The first time Japanese soldier Hiroo Onoda accepted that World War II was over was in 1974, when Onoda's commanding officer flew to Lubang Island. Onoda had hidden there since 1945, when the war ended.

Tuy Hoa

CAMBODIA

Work first began on the Angkor Wat temple in the early 1300s. The huge temple was built for King Suryavaraman II.

Mactan Island

In 1520 Ferdinand Magellan's ships were the first to round Cape Horn and reach the Pacific Ocean from the Atlantic. He named the ocean "Pacific," which means peaceful. Magellan died on Mactan Island.

Mount Apo
△

Rafflesia plants were first discovered in Indonesia in 1818. The largest species has the world's biggest flower—more than one yard across. Its smell of rotting meat attracts the flies that pollinate the plant.

Jerudong Park

BANDAR SERI BEGAWAN

BRUNEI

The world's first free amusement park, Jerudong Park, was opened in 1994 in Brunei.

MALAYSIA

The first live Komodo dragons were caught by W. Douglas Burdon in 1926. At 13 ft. (4m) long, the Komodo dragon is the world's largest lizard.

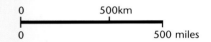

British forces in India first planted experimental tea plantations in Darjeeling in 1841. The region now produces about 10,000 tons of tea every year.

akatoa

AKARTA

Komodo Island

In May 2002 East Timor became independent and the first new nation of the 21st century.

INDONESIA

EAST TIMOR ■**DILI**

0 ——————— 500km

0 ——————— 500 miles

China and Japan

China is one of the oldest countries in the world, and it was the first country to have a population of more than one billion people. Japan is made up of four large islands and more than 3,000 smaller ones. About one-tenth of the world's active volcanoes are in Japan.

Urumqi is about 1,550 mi. (2,500km) away from the ocean, farther than any other city in the world. About 2.9 million people live there.

Marco Polo was not the first European to visit the Mongol empire. The Italian Giovanni da Pian del Carpine reached the capital of Karakorum in 1246.

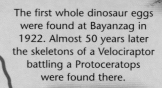

The first whole dinosaur eggs were found at Bayanzag in 1922. Almost 50 years later the skeletons of a Velociraptor battling a Protoceratops were found there.

Karakorum

Bayanzag

China's first nuclear weapon was tested at Lop Nur in 1964. The bomb was the first of more than 40 nuclear weapon tests at Lop Nur.

Urumqi

Jiuquan

The world's oldest noodles were found in Lajia in 2005. They were made of millet grain and are 4,000 years old.

Lop Nur

In 2003 astronaut Yang Liwei blasted off on board a Shenzhou-5 spacecraft in China's first manned space flight.

CHINA

Golmud

Lajia

The Terracotta Army was first discovered by local farmers in 1974. This amazing collection of 7,000 clay soldiers with clay chariots and 500 horses was buried with the Emperor of Qin near Xi'an in 210 B.C.

The first train ran from Beijing to Tibet in 2006. The Qinghai-Tibet railroad, which starts at Golmud, is one of the highest in the world, with some tracks more than 3 mi. (5km) above sea level.

Plateau of Tibet

The first live giant panda brought to the west was Su-Lin, captured by Ruth Harkness in the mountains northwest of Chengdu in 1936.

Gangkar Puensum

BHUTAN

Chengdu

Gangkar Puensum in Bhutan is the world's highest unclimbed mountain. It is about 24,835 ft. (7,570m) high and has not been scaled because the Bhutan government forbids it.

The magnificent Potala Palace in Lhasa, Tibet, was completed in the 1600s and was the traditional home of the Dalai Lama, the leader of Tibetan Buddhists. It has 1,000 rooms, about 200,000 statues, and 10,000 altars.

In 1948 a Catalina flying boat traveling from Macao to Hong Kong became the first plane to be hijacked in the air. Only the hijackers' leader survived the subsequent crash.

0 ——— 500km
0 ——— 500 miles

Mongolia's biggest festival is Naadam, held in the capital city of Ulan Bator. Horseracing, Mongolian wrestling, and archery are the main events.

Construction of the first hotel to have seven revolving restaurants began in 1987, but the hotel has never been finished.

The first trains to cross the border between North and South Korea since 1950 ran in 2007.

The world's biggest firework exploded over Lake Toya in 1988. It weighed 1,543 lbs. (700kg) and its light display was 0.75 mi. (1.2km) wide.

■ ULAN BATOR

MONGOLIA

Work on the Forbidden City (now in Beijing) began in 1406. It is circled by a giant moat and 23-ft. (7m)-high walls and houses the palaces of more than 20 Chinese emperors.

The first seismometer was invented by the Chinese scientist Zhang Heng in A.D. 132. His copper urn could detect earthquakes many miles away.

The first time people of 50 different nationalities shared a sauna was in 2007 at the Yuraiya Sauna and Bath House.

Lake Toya

Danica Patrick became the first woman to win an Indy race when she won the Indy Japan 300 at the Twin Ring Motegi circuit in April 2008.

BEIJING ■

NORTH KOREA

PYONGYANG

The first commercial mp3 player was the MPMan F10 launched in 1998.

Panmunjom
■ SEOUL
SOUTH KOREA

Nagaoka
Motegi

Luoyang

TOKYO
Hamamatsu

JAPAN

Daegu

Osaka

Qufu

Three Gorges Dam

The quickest goal scored in a soccer World Cup finals match was at Daegu in 2002. Turkey's Hakan Sukur struck just 11 seconds after kickoff.

Saga

The first Shinkansen high speed train service began running from Tokyo to Osaka in 1964, halving the journey time.

The world's first portable music player, the Walkman, was invented by Sony engineers in 1979.

The great Chinese thinker Confucius was born in Qufu around 551 B.C. The temple complex honoring him is the second-largest in China.

The world's longest sushi roll was made in Saga in 2002 from 2,205 lbs. (1,000kg) of rice and 10,000 sheets of seaweed. It measured 5,988 ft. (1,825m).

Work first began on the Three Gorges Dam in 1994. When completed in 2011, the 1.4-mi. (2.3km)-long dam will generate more hydroelectricity than any other dam.

Shuri

Michio Suzuki's company began making weaving looms in 1909. In 1952 it produced the Power Free motorcycle, and it is now the world's 12th-largest motor vehicle maker.

Keelung

TAIPEI
TAIWAN

Hong Kong

Macao

Taiwan's National Palace Museum first opened in 1965 to display some of the 600,000 pieces of Chinese art Chiang Kai Shek took to Keelung from mainland China in 1949.

The first movie Jackie Chan made was *Big and Little Wong Tin Bar*, filmed in Hong Kong in 1962. Chan has now starred in more than 100 movies.

Karate was first taught secretly on the island of Okinawa. The founder of the Shokotan school of karate, Gichin Funakoshi, grew up in Shuri.

41

Australia and New Zealand

Australia was first settled by Aboriginal peoples from the north between 50,000 and 70,000 years ago. It is the largest landmass in the Pacific Ocean. New Zealand is about 995 mi. (1,600km) to the southeast. Thousands of smaller islands are dotted through the Pacific, including Fiji, Tonga, and the Solomon Islands.

PAPUA NEW GUINEA

The first south-to-north crossing of Australia was by the Burke and Wills expedition in 1860. They traveled 1,740 mi. (2,800km) to within 3 mi. (5km) of the Gulf of Carpentaria. All but one of the 19 explorers died.

Darwin

Kakadu

Gulf of Carpentaria

0 — 500km

0 — 500 miles

The first major attack on Australia in World War II was in 1942, when the Japanese fleet attacked the city of Darwin with 188 planes.

The first Aboriginal settlers arrived in the Kakadu region about 40,000 years ago. Kakadu became a national park in 1975 and has 5,000 Aboriginal rock paintings.

Julia Creek

The first flying doctor service began in 1928 when a De Havilland DH 50 flew to Julia Creek. Today the Royal Flying Doctor Service of Australia has 36 aircraft serving isolated areas.

Port Hedland

AUSTRALIA

The longest-ever freight train had 682 cars carrying iron ore to Port Hedland. The train was 24,124 ft. (7,353m) long and was pushed by eight locomotives!

Opals were first discovered in Coober Pedy in 1915. Today many residents live in underground homes there to escape the searing summer heat.

The oldest Australian-made car still running is the 1899 Shearer Steam Carriage, built at Mannum.

Coober Pedy

The first settlement in Australia for free people, rather than convicts and soldiers, was Perth. It was founded by British settlers in 1829 as the capital of the Swan River Colony.

Eucla

Mannum

Port Adelaide

EUCLA

NORSEMAN 712 km   495 CEDUNA

MELBOURNE 1,989 km

SYDNEY 2,522 km

BRISBANE 2,980 km

Perth

Archie Thompson became the first soccer player to score 13 times in a World Cup qualifying game at Coff's Harbour stadium in 2001. The final score was a world record as Australia beat American Samoa 31–0.

The handful of people who live in the remote town of Eucla live in their own time zone, 45 minutes ahead of Western Australia and 45 minutes behind South Australia.

The first camel in Australia was called Harry. He traveled from Tenerife, in the Canary Islands, to Port Adelaide in 1840.

Cane toads were first brought to Australia from Hawaii in 1935 to eat cane beetles. Just 102 toads were released near Cairns. Today there are more than two billion.

The first underwater post office opened in 2003. Visitors can buy waterproof postcards on Vanuatu and mail them 164 ft. (50m) offshore.

Fiji played their first rugby union international against Samoa in 1924 at 7 A.M.—so their opponents could go to work afterward.

The last place in the world where rocks were used as money (called rai) was the island of Yap. Some stones measure 13 ft. (4m) across!

Pacific Islands

VANUATU

FIJI ISLANDS

SAMOA TONGA

Yap Island

Papeete

Cairns

A message in a bottle thrown into the ocean from the SS *Arawatta* in 1910 was first read in 1983, when it was picked up on Moreton Island.

Taufa'ahau Tupou IV first became King of Tonga in 1965 and ruled for 41 years. He became the world's heaviest monarch in the 1970s.

Conrad Hall was born in Papeete and became the first person from Tahiti to win an Oscar. He won in cinematography for *Butch Cassidy and the Sundance Kid* in 1969.

Famous cricketer Donald Bradman made his first century (100 runs in an inning) for Bowral Public School against Mittagong when he was 12.

Easter Island's amazing Moai statues were first carved out of solid rock around A.D. 800. There are more than 880 Moai, and the largest is about 69 ft. (21m) tall and weighs around 300 tons .

Moreton Island

The first woman to pilot a glider was Florence Taylor, who flew her husband's homemade glider along Narrabeen Beach in 1909.

Escapologist Harry Houdini was the first person to fly an aircraft in Australia. He made three flights in his Voisin biplane at Diggers Rest in 1910.

The first Zorb was invented by brothers David and Andrew Akers in 1994. The giant clear plastic ball with a rider inside rolls downhill up at to 31 mph (50km/h).

Gisborne was the first city in the world to welcome the new millennium. Its Maori name, Tairawhiti, means "the place where the sun rises."

Narrabeen

Bowral

Auckland

CANBERRA
Diggers Rest

The first European to see New Zealand was the Dutch sailor Abel Tasman, who sighted New Zealand's South Island in December 1642.

Gisborne

Melbourne

In 1969 the first TV images of men on the Moon were broadcast around the world. Many of the images of the *Apollo 11* mission were transmitted from the Honeysuckle Creek tracking station, near Canberra.

Golden Bay

The first pavlova (a meringue with cream and fruit) was made in 1926 by a chef in Wellington for the Russian ballerina Anna Pavlova, who was touring New Zealand.

WELLINGTON

Tasmania
Hobart

The last known Tasmanian tiger, called Benjamin, died in Hobart Zoo in 1936.

NEW ZEALAND

The first permanent bungee jumping site was the 141-ft. (43m)-long Kawarau Bridge Bungy in Queenstown, which opened in 1988.

The first full-length feature film to be made was *The Story of the Kelly Gang*, which premiered at the Athenaeum Hall, Melbourne, in 1906.

Queenstown

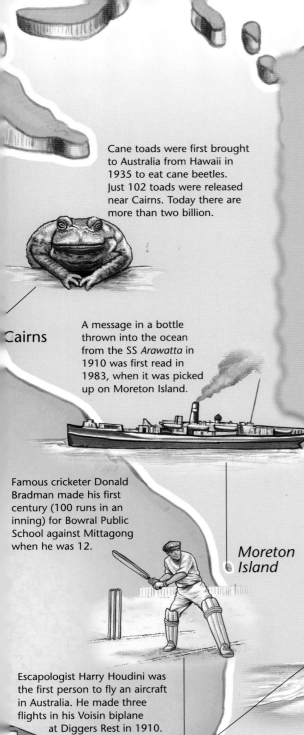

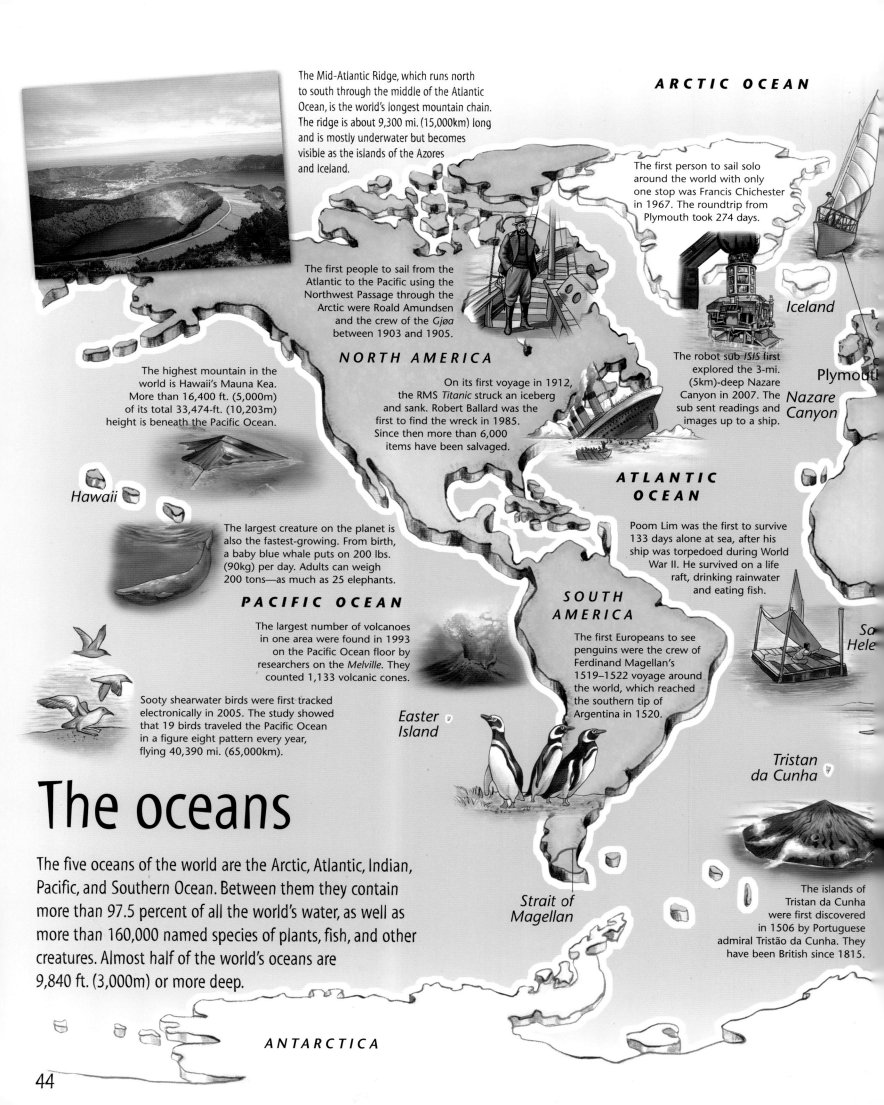

The Mid-Atlantic Ridge, which runs north to south through the middle of the Atlantic Ocean, is the world's longest mountain chain. The ridge is about 9,300 mi. (15,000km) long and is mostly underwater but becomes visible as the islands of the Azores and Iceland.

The first person to sail solo around the world with only one stop was Francis Chichester in 1967. The roundtrip from Plymouth took 274 days.

The first people to sail from the Atlantic to the Pacific using the Northwest Passage through the Arctic were Roald Amundsen and the crew of the *Gjøa* between 1903 and 1905.

Iceland

NORTH AMERICA

On its first voyage in 1912, the RMS *Titanic* struck an iceberg and sank. Robert Ballard was the first to find the wreck in 1985. Since then more than 6,000 items have been salvaged.

The robot sub *ISIS* first explored the 3-mi. (5km)-deep Nazare Canyon in 2007. The sub sent readings and images up to a ship.

Plymouth

Nazare Canyon

The highest mountain in the world is Hawaii's Mauna Kea. More than 16,400 ft. (5,000m) of its total 33,474-ft. (10,203m) height is beneath the Pacific Ocean.

ATLANTIC OCEAN

Hawaii

The largest creature on the planet is also the fastest-growing. From birth, a baby blue whale puts on 200 lbs. (90kg) per day. Adults can weigh 200 tons—as much as 25 elephants.

Poom Lim was the first to survive 133 days alone at sea, after his ship was torpedoed during World War II. He survived on a life raft, drinking rainwater and eating fish.

PACIFIC OCEAN

SOUTH AMERICA

The largest number of volcanoes in one area were found in 1993 on the Pacific Ocean floor by researchers on the *Melville*. They counted 1,133 volcanic cones.

The first Europeans to see penguins were the crew of Ferdinand Magellan's 1519–1522 voyage around the world, which reached the southern tip of Argentina in 1520.

Sa Hele

Sooty shearwater birds were first tracked electronically in 2005. The study showed that 19 birds traveled the Pacific Ocean in a figure eight pattern every year, flying 40,390 mi. (65,000km).

Easter Island

Tristan da Cunha

The oceans

The five oceans of the world are the Arctic, Atlantic, Indian, Pacific, and Southern Ocean. Between them they contain more than 97.5 percent of all the world's water, as well as more than 160,000 named species of plants, fish, and other creatures. Almost half of the world's oceans are 9,840 ft. (3,000m) or more deep.

Strait of Magellan

The islands of Tristan da Cunha were first discovered in 1506 by Portuguese admiral Tristão da Cunha. They have been British since 1815.

ANTARCTICA

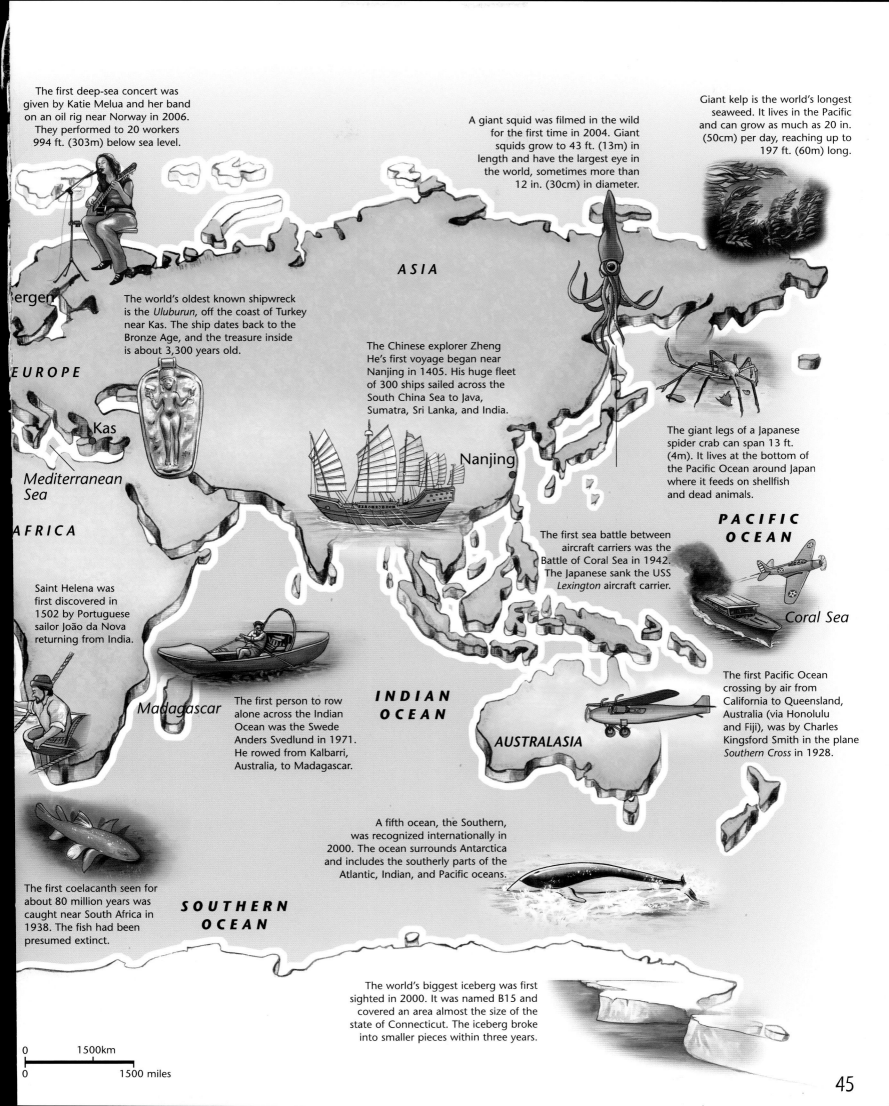

The first deep-sea concert was given by Katie Melua and her band on an oil rig near Norway in 2006. They performed to 20 workers 994 ft. (303m) below sea level.

A giant squid was filmed in the wild for the first time in 2004. Giant squids grow to 43 ft. (13m) in length and have the largest eye in the world, sometimes more than 12 in. (30cm) in diameter.

Giant kelp is the world's longest seaweed. It lives in the Pacific and can grow as much as 20 in. (50cm) per day, reaching up to 197 ft. (60m) long.

ASIA

Bergen

The world's oldest known shipwreck is the *Uluburun*, off the coast of Turkey near Kas. The ship dates back to the Bronze Age, and the treasure inside is about 3,300 years old.

The Chinese explorer Zheng He's first voyage began near Nanjing in 1405. His huge fleet of 300 ships sailed across the South China Sea to Java, Sumatra, Sri Lanka, and India.

EUROPE

Kas

Nanjing

The giant legs of a Japanese spider crab can span 13 ft. (4m). It lives at the bottom of the Pacific Ocean around Japan where it feeds on shellfish and dead animals.

Mediterranean Sea

AFRICA

PACIFIC OCEAN

The first sea battle between aircraft carriers was the Battle of Coral Sea in 1942. The Japanese sank the USS *Lexington* aircraft carrier.

Saint Helena was first discovered in 1502 by Portuguese sailor João da Nova returning from India.

Coral Sea

The first Pacific Ocean crossing by air from California to Queensland, Australia (via Honolulu and Fiji), was by Charles Kingsford Smith in the plane *Southern Cross* in 1928.

Madagascar

The first person to row alone across the Indian Ocean was the Swede Anders Svedlund in 1971. He rowed from Kalbarri, Australia, to Madagascar.

INDIAN OCEAN

AUSTRALASIA

A fifth ocean, the Southern, was recognized internationally in 2000. The ocean surrounds Antarctica and includes the southerly parts of the Atlantic, Indian, and Pacific oceans.

The first coelacanth seen for about 80 million years was caught near South Africa in 1938. The fish had been presumed extinct.

SOUTHERN OCEAN

The world's biggest iceberg was first sighted in 2000. It was named B15 and covered an area almost the size of the state of Connecticut. The iceberg broke into smaller pieces within three years.

0   1500km

0   1500 miles

45

Lewis Gordon Pugh became the first person to make a long-distance swim at the North Pole in July 2007. He swam 0.62 mi. (1km) in 19 minutes in freezing water.

Steven Spielberg's first blockbuster was *Jaws*, filmed on Martha's Vineyard, Massachusetts. It won three Oscars, inspired three sequels and earned more than $470 million.

Index

Ludwig von Bersuda first thought of the sport of underwater rugby in 1961. The first tournament was held at a swimming pool in Müellheim, Germany, in 1965.

The first Viking raid on England was in A.D. 793. Vikings from Norway attacked the monastery at Lindesfarne, looted its valuables, and killed or captured many monks.

The world's first underwater hotel, Hydropolis, is in Dubai. It has 220 luxury suites under 66 ft. (20m) of water.

46

Remy Bricka was the first person to walk across the Atlantic on ski floats. He went from Tenerife to Trinidad, arriving in May 1998.

In 1774 Constantine Phipps was the first European to describe a polar bear in a book about his attempt to reach the North Pole.

Europe's longest bridge was opened to traffic in 1998. Portugal's Vasco da Gama Bridge measures 56,387 ft. (17,185m) in length.

Surrealist painter Salvador Dalí first returned to his home town of Figueres, Spain, after being expelled from Madrid's San Fernando School of Fine Arts in 1926.

The first underwater post office opened in 2003. Visitors can buy waterproof postcards on Vanuatu and mail them 164 ft. (50m) offshore.

Acknowledgments

The publisher would like to thank the following for permission to reproduce their material. Every care has been taken to trace copyright holders. However, if there have been unintentional omissions or failure to trace copyright holders, we apologize and will, if informed, endeavor to make corrections in any future edition.

top = *t*; bottom = *b*; center = *c*; left = *l*; right = *r*

page 2 Alamy/Phil Rees; 3 Shutterstock/Jeff Schultes; 4 Reuters; 4 Photolibrary/Age Fotostock; 5*tr* Corbis/Troy Wayrynen; 5*bc* Art Archive/Alfredo Dagli Orti; 7*t* Corbis/Bettman; 7*b* Getty Images/MPI; 8 Reuters/Gary Hershorn; 9 Ronald Grant Archive/Walt Disney Inc.; 11 Getty Images/AFP; 12*t* Getty Images/Digital Vision; 12*c* Bridgeman Art Library/British Museum; 13 Getty Images/Tom Shaw; 14*t* Naturepl/Nature Production; 14*c* Reuters/Eliseo Fernandez; 16 Corbis/Wolfgang Rattay; 17 Science Photo Library/CNRI; 18*br* PA/AP/Stew Milne; 20*t* Getty/Allsport; 20*b* Alamy/Pictorial Press; 23 Art Archive/Nasjonal Galleriet, Oslo; 24 Getty Images/Carlos Alvarez; 25 Getty Images/Bongarts; 26 Corbis/Lars Halbauer; 27 Art Archive/ Museo Capitolino, Rome/Dagli Orti; 29*t* Rex/Richard Gardner; 29*c* Unicef; 30*b* Getty Images/Milos Bicanski; Art Archive/Gianni Dagli Orti; 33*cl* Art Archive/V&A Museum; 33*cr* Shutterstock/Svetlana Chernova; 33*b* Corbis/George Hall; 34*t* Rex Features; 34*c* Getty Images/Lonely Planet; 36*t* Getty Images/Karim Sahib/AFP; 36*c* Photolibrary/Jon Arnold; 37 Photolibrary/Guiziou Franck; 39*l* Shutterstock/Juriah Mosin; 39*r* Photolibrary/Luca Invernizzi Tettoni; 39*b* Corbis/Robert Harding; 40 Shutterstock/Gleb Vinnikov; 41 Shutterstock/Qing Ding; 42 Getty Images/Darren England; 43 Photolibrary/Angelo Cavalli; 44 Shutterstock/Ricardo A. Alves

Illustrations by Planman Technologies (India) Pvt. Ltd.

In 1970, *Lunokhod-1* became the first remote-controlled robot to land on another body in the solar system. It traveled 6.5 mi. (10.5km) around the Moon's surface, beaming back more than 20,000 photographs to Earth.

The first successful landing on Mars occurred in 1976. *Viking 1* had a robot arm and continued working until 1982.

MARS

Neil Armstrong became the first person to step on to the Moon on July 21, 1969, during the *Apollo 11* mission.

MOON

Mars's moons, Deimos and Phobos, were discovered in 1877 by Aspeth Hall at the U.S. Naval Observatory.

The Soviet satellite *Luna 2* was the first man-made object to land on the Moon in 1959, ten years before the Apollo Moon landings.

EARTH

The first and only person to play golf on the Moon was Alan Shepard during the 1971 *Apollo 14* mission. He used a six iron swung in one hand.

The first sandwich was eaten in space by Virgil "Gus" Grissom, who smuggled a corned beef sandwich onboard the *Gemini 3* spacecraft in 1965.